Before I Forget
A Family Memoir

Brian Tesler

Before I Forget

ISBN 978-0-9554515-0-8
ISBN 0-9554515-0-7

First published in Great Britain by Mind Advertising Ltd
Production and design by Mind Advertising

beforeiforget@mind-advertising.com

Printed and bound by Biddles, Norfolk

For Stella, David and the past.
To Nicola, Francesca, Isabella and the future.

Acknowledgements

Alan Grace's The Link With Home – 60 Years Of Forces Radio refreshed my memories of the Radio Station in Trieste. For many of the details of London's life during the Second World War, and of the progress of the War itself, I am indebted to The World At War by Mark Arnold-Foster and London At War by Joanna Mack & Steve Humphries. Both books are associated with fine documentary series produced by my programme departments at Thames Television and London Weekend Television respectively. Some of the details of the family story I owe to my sister Rosalind Clayton and my cousin Denise Bogush. Without my son Simon's initial impulse and sustained expertise the project would have neither begun nor continued. And without my wife Audrey's patient encouragement it would not have concluded. I am grateful to them all.

Before I Forget

Family Beginnings

Something's Coming

School Days

Growing Up

What Happened Next?

Before I Forget

Why didn't I write things down?

My father came to this country as a boy of fifteen in the middle of the First World War, not speaking a word of English. Ten years later he was a fully integrated Londoner; and he and the young woman who was to become my mother were living in an East End of London that was stylish and colourful, full of smart shops, cinemas, theatres and dancehalls, bustling with life. Like my father, my mother and her four sisters – the five Hyman girls – were part of the East End's vibrant Jewish community of the early decades of the last century, long gone and only dimly remembered. Why didn't I ask my parents and my aunts and uncles about those days while they were still alive, and write their memories down? I can remember sitting with my friend Jackie Shafron in his family kitchen at the age of eight, the two of us working on some elaborate construction with Jackie's Meccano set, when his mother suddenly asked me "What do you want to be when you grow up?" "A writer" I said.

So why didn't I write?

I can never recapture my parents' memories now, except indirectly and hazily through family photographs accumulated over the years. But what I can do, before I forget, is write down my own memories: memories of the East End, of my parents and grandparents, of my childhood experience before, during and after the Second World War. The fact that they are my own memories means that they will be very self-centred – all of them, essentially, about me. But, as one of my grand-daughters at the age of seven used to say, with her arms stretched wide and her shoulders hunched in a comprehensive shrug: "So?" They might at least give Nicola, Francesca and Isabella some idea of what it was like to be a youngster in London sixty or seventy years ago; some impression of the kind of people their great-grandparents were; some sense of the sort of life that was lived in the last century in peacetime and in war.

It was another time, my dears, another place, another world.

Family Beginnings

Stella

My mother was born Esther Hyman on 27 October 1902 in Whitechapel Hospital, in the District of Mile End Old Town. "Stella" probably came from one of her younger sisters' attempts to pronounce her name; whatever its origin, Esther preferred it and was known as Stella for the rest of her 101 years.

Betty, the romantic one of Stella's sisters, never ceased telling her daughter Denise about the family's history. Alas, cousin Denise didn't write anything down either, but she remembers Betty saying that her mother, Yetta Himovitch, was an innkeeper's daughter in Russia and her father, Harris Hyman, a travelling salesman. They met, fell in love (remember, this is the romantic daughter telling it) and married in Russia some time around 1889. Annie, Stella's elder sister, was born in 1891, and the little family came to England about two years later.

Putting together pieces of the jigsaw passed on by Denise from Aunt Betty, there were twins between Annie and Stella, Sam and Rose, born in London some time in the late 1890s. Rose died as a baby; Sam was killed at the age of eighteen fighting for Britain in the First World War. There was also another brother, Alf, a good-looking young man I can just about remember, who must have been born around the turn of the century in England.

Whatever it was that Harris had been selling in Russia, by the time Stella was born he had turned to the bakery business. Stella's birth certificate gives his profession in 1902 as Journeyman Baker, so he was working for somebody else at that time. It also gives his signature as a cross – "the mark of Harris Hyman" – evidently he hadn't yet got round to writing in English. In 1902, the family was living at No 40 Nelson Street, right in the middle of the bustling main roads whose names are for me still redolent of London's East End: Commercial Road, Whitechapel Road, Mile End Road.

Harris learned his new trade well. By the time Stella was a young girl he owned two baker's shops not far from each other in Globe Road, a little north of Nelson Street; and Stella and two of the sisters who followed her – Pearl, born in 1905, and Betty, born in 1907 – worked in one or other of them full time when they left school.

Annie married at the age of 18 and had a home of her own to look after. Eve, the last of the Hyman Girls, came along in 1912 and seems not to have worked in either of the bakeries.

Harris worked very hard according to Aunt Betty, and that was what killed him. He used to make his way between the two shops very early in the morning, supervising and participating in the baking of each day's fresh bread, going each winter from the oven-heat of one bakery to the other, through the bitter cold of London's early morning streets – not the wisest thing to do for someone who appears to have been prone to bronchitis anyway. He died in Whitechapel Hospital in 1935 at the age of 66. I remember visiting him there when I was six years old, and it's the only memory I have of him.

David

My father came to England with his father, Gershon, in 1916. He was fifteen years old. How they got here in the middle of a world war, unable to speak a word of English; how they made their way to London's East End, a twenty minute walk from the docks, found somewhere to live, brought my grandmother Sophie over from Baremel', their village in the Ukraine, set up home and made a living from absolutely nothing, has to be a fascinating story. You would think, wouldn't you, that I would have asked them about it years later? All I remember being told is that David and Gershon made a living at first by selling things from a barrow – *what things?* – and were eventually taken on as piece-workers in a millinery factory. There, David developed sufficient expertise to become a full-time machinist in an industry that boomed after the First World War, when every woman of whatever class wore hats; and ladies' millinery became his lifelong business.

Unfortunately, there is no Cousin or Aunt or any other relative on my father's side of the family to feed me scraps of information about the Teslers. Tesler itself doesn't sound particularly Russian or Jewish but it appears not to be an abbreviation of something like Teslerovitch. I used to think it was a Western Immigration Officer's transcription of Tesla, a well-established name in the Balkans whose borders are very near Baremel': Nikola Tesla was a renowned 19th century electrical engineer born in Croatia who, among many other things, invented fluorescent lighting, developed the alternating current electrical supply system and had a unit of magnetic density named after him.

If the Teslers had come out of that sort of stock they left their technical genes well behind before they got to me. However, it transpires from my son Simon's

Google research that Tesler, spelt exactly that way, is a surname quite common among Eastern European Jews; Tesla appears to be essentially a Christian name, and is unrelated.

When I was a lad we knew of only one other Tesler: Simcha, a smiling, affable man who was an Orthodox Rabbi and some sort of relative of my father. He officiated at my Barmitzvah lunch, and I still have the copy of Cecil Roth's history of The Jewish Contribution To Civilisation he presented to me to mark the occasion, warmly dedicated on the inside cover and wishing me A Very Hearty Mazel Tov, "From a Tesler to a Tesler, London, March 1st 1942".

I seem to remember that there had been an elder brother of my father who died fighting for the Russian Czar in World War One. Perhaps that was in 1916 and was the final spur for Gershon and his family to seek another life in England. Ironically, the name Gershon in Hebrew denotes "a stranger in a strange land". He certainly seems to have been that. I remember him as a mild and kindly man who only ever worked with or for my father; a quiet, rather ineffectual pipe-smoker just coasting along in England. There was a family legend that in Baremel' he had been the village strong man – what does a village strong man *do*? – and certainly, in the photographs that remain of his life in Russia, he seems a powerful, handsome, confident *mensch*, with an impressive imperial moustache. In England, the photographs show that fine moustache diminishing as he himself appears to do, until the moustache disappears completely and he becomes just the nice, kind old Jewish grandfather – the Zaida – who used to take me for walks in Victoria Park when I was a little boy.

The family was clearly not a lowly peasant one, for all Gershon's strong man status. Sophie, his wife, also looks rather grand in her Russian photographs: stately, dark and mysterious, a power-dressing matriarch sporting rimless glasses, or are they pince-nez? And then she comes to England, the glasses become horn-rimmed, and she is transformed into the gentle and benign Jewish grandmother, the classic Booba; in her case, *Big* Booba: not only because in time that will be one way of distinguishing her from the other grandmother, the diminutive Yetta, who will inevitably become Little Booba, but because that's what dear Sophie is: plump, stately, cuddly: *big*.

Stella And David

How and where did they meet, Stella and David?

They married in 1927 so they came across each other some time in the mid-

1920s. By then, London's East End had grown and begun to flourish along with the rest of post-war England. It was no longer an immigrant ghetto of sweat-shop workers and teeming communities of ramshackle homes and tenement buildings. There was plenty of work, if you were bright and enterprising enough to find it. There were elegant streets and houses, fashionable shops and convenience stores, smart cafes and tea-rooms (where the older customers drank their lemon tea Russian style, through a lump of sugar gripped between the teeth); there were cinemas and theatres, and many restaurants, reflecting the different cuisines brought to London by the thousands of Jewish immigrants who had found their way from Russia, Central and Eastern Europe and the Middle East to England and had not gone on to make the longer journey to New York.

Until they anglicised themselves, as most of them strove to do, Yiddish was the Jewish East Enders' common language, a language evolved from German and Hebrew with some Serb, Baltic and Russian thrown in for spice. In London, as in New York, there were newspapers in Yiddish, books and magazines in Yiddish, screen captions in cinemas in Yiddish, plays in Yiddish performed in Yiddish theatres. I can remember my father regularly reading Yiddish newspapers – from back to front and right to left of course, as one reads Hebrew: Yiddish is written in Hebrew characters.

The only bound volumes in our house when I was a small boy were the works of Sholem Aleichem, a famous Jewish storyteller; Aleichem's name was printed in English on the binding but, inside, the works themselves were in Yiddish. I know that there were at least two major Yiddish theatres in the East End, one of them The Grand Palais. My mother and father used to go there sometimes on Sunday afternoons; now and again they took me with them, and though I couldn't understand a word, the uproarious, over-the-top hyper-theatricality of the proceedings totally mesmerised me.

Is that where they met? At a theatre? In a cinema? In a coffee-house? At a dance? At any of these or the other places where girls and boys still usually meet each other today? – though not, for most Jewish boys and girls in those days, perhaps not even now – in a pub? I'm told that once in a throwaway remark Stella said that she and Dave had met at a dance "in the West End".

They must have cut quite a dash. They were both young and good-looking and snappily dressed. David had probably become Dave by now: it had a more relaxed, contemporary sound and by the time I could remember such details he was never addressed as anything else. He was doing well as a trusted lieutenant in the millinery business, working for a big wholesaler named Collins; Stella was one of the young Jewish Princesses helping out in the prosperous bakeries owned by their hardworking father. Look at the clothes and accessories in their contemporary photographs: Stella with her chic Japanese parasol and her white stockings, Dave no longer the aspiring Russian late-teenager in his formal dark three-piece suit and homburg hat: now he's the dashing young Englishman with the white tennis sweater and shoes, his tweedy sports jacket complemented by a white pocket handkerchief , his jaunty flat cap pulled well down over his forehead, strolling along the promenade of Westcliff or Margate.

Perhaps that's where they first caught sight of each other: at the seaside, on a weekend day by the sea: that's where the boys and girls used to go, mob-handed, on a Sunday. There's Dave and three of his mates, two of them with walking canes – how smart! – one of them with a raincoat: it looks as if there's going to be a bit of rain before they come up against Stella and her girl-friends, a gang of seven in a glamorous line sweeping down the prom – you can see that they've turned the head of at least one young male as they go.

The seaside features heavily in Dave and Stella's courtship: there are the two of them cuddling up on a rug spread out on another downcast beach, though they seem blissfully unaware of the weather; there's Dave on his knees, begging for some favour or another; there's Dave again, rather formally dressed for a beach party, complete with collar and tie, holding up a little message for Stella which you can just make out says "I LOVE YOU"; there are the two of them, much more smartly casual, having their photograph taken in a photographer's studio in Margate. It looks quite serious. And it is: Dave and Stella are married on the 12th of June 1927. He's twenty-six, she's twenty-five.

Married Life

It was a pretty slap-up do, according to the photographs. Dave is in dinner jacket and glossy top hat, complete with wing-collar, gloves and spats; Stella and her bridesmaids – her three as yet unmarried sisters – are resplendent in their glamorously fashionable short dresses and enormous floral bouquets. Harris has obviously done them proud – and he had three more daughters' weddings to look forward to: it was just as well that the bakery business was flourishing.

I came along twenty months later, in February 1929, and my sister Rosalind arrived four years after that in April 1933, so I had the field to myself for my first four years. The photographs show that I was a beautiful baby – for about eight months. I then became very fat, with a mop of dark hair and a great moon face with an open-mouthed, half-witted expression plastered on it. Rosalind was also a beautiful baby, but she stayed beautiful: a little china doll to my butterball.

According to my birth certificate, we were living at 231 Burdett Road when I was born, a major thoroughfare stretching from Mile End Road to Commercial Road completing a kind of East End Triangle, so we were still in the very heart of the East End. It must have been rented accommodation, a flat of some kind; I have vague recollections of large dark rooms and lino-covered floors.

My earliest conscious memory is of being potty-trained in such a room, at the age of – what? eighteen months? two years? I can hear my father urging me to "*Do* something, there's a good boy"; and I can remember trying very hard, and being lifted off and wiped, my mother calling out "Did he do anything?" and my father looking into the chamberpot and saying "No, just a little fart"; I remember looking into the pot myself and there at the bottom of it was a little speck of faeces. I remember thinking for far too many years afterwards that this was what a fart was: a tiny little turd.

Rosalind's Birth Certificate gives her place of birth as Kyverdale Road, Stoke Newington, in North London, but, after a little detective work from Cousin Denise, I understand that this was most likely the address of a nursing home (Denise's Birth Certificate gives her own birth address as the Middlesex Hospital) because I'm certain the family was out of the East End proper by 1933, the year of Rosalind's birth, and living in Walthamstow.

I say I'm certain because I have a clear memory of being taken in a push-chair as a very small child to a less than half-built street, full of workmen and clatter and machinery, my mother wheeling me along wooden planks past the gaping foundations of houses in the course of construction, about which I could sense she and my father were very excited. This embryonic street was Markmanor Avenue, a brand new building development to which we must have moved not long afterwards because I have distinct memories of our house as a toddler and we were clearly well ensconced there by the time I started my elementary education a few streets away in Sybourn Street, at the statutory age of five.

Walthamstow is about as far north of Whitechapel as Fulham is to the west of it, and in the early thirties I suppose they were about the same kind of inner suburban London, vastly different from the noise and bustle of East End or West End. Markmanor Avenue was a pleasant, airy little cul-de-sac of around fifty semi-detached houses. It was certainly a move upward for the Teslers, and we were to live there until the Blitz drove us out in 1940.

Markmanor Avenue

There is one surviving photograph of the exterior of No 44 Markmanor Avenue.

It must have been taken around 1935 because standing in front of the house is a little two-year old Rosalind, holding the hand of our Welsh maid Winnie. The house is mostly brick, with a little mock-Tudor timbering and stucco on the façade; it has a wooden fence with a white wooden gate – though the fence was replaced later by a medium-high stone or brick wall because I remember pushing Rosalind off it one time and being whacked as a result by my father with the rolled-up comics he used to bring home for me on a Friday night on his way back from work.

The house had a little garden at the front and a garden at the back that was really quite large – or so it seems in my recollection and, still, in my dreams. It had a well-manicured lawn, with a crazy-paving path down the middle; a trellis arch with some kind of greenery climbing up it; a variety of plants and shrubs and flowers round the borders; and a vegetable garden: I was no more interested in vegetables then than I am now, so I only remember peas and wild strawberries growing there. At the very bottom of the garden, and running along the back of all the houses on our side of the Avenue, was a thick, high privet hedge and on the other side of that a little stream, beyond which was a line of trees.

There is one surviving photograph of the back garden, with me at the age of six on a smart little tricycle and Winnie in her full maid's regalia of black uniform, white cap, apron and cuffs. The photo shows some of the lawn (complete with deck-chair and sun-umbrella), and the path, the borders and the back-drop of trees. It's all really rather rural. Surprisingly, it was my father who was the enthusiastic gardener – though, come to think of it, it isn't really all that surprising: later on, during and after the war, he had an allotment which he diligently tended for years: he was after all a country boy and had been brought up in a little village himself.

According to the Greater London Street Atlas, the area around Markmanor Avenue is still undeveloped: it sits isolated in the middle of a great expanse lying to the east, west and north of it, broken only by a line of filter beds – presumably belonging to the Water Authority – and an area marked as allotments.

For me and my friends that space was one huge playground of fields and trees and bushes, with the filter beds and the little streams that ran between them providing water hazards to leap or slosh through. We built hideaways and dens in the undergrowth, strode manfully across the fields singing cowboy songs we'd heard on the radio, climbed trees – yes, even I climbed trees, until I lost my hold of one insecure bough and fell flat and very painfully on my back. And the water hazards could be genuinely hazardous: crossing one of the streams, little Davy Suzmann trod on some broken glass; the glass pierced the plimsoll he was wearing, the cut became infected, and he died a few weeks later of septicaemia.

Poor Davy: penicillin would have saved him today. And yet, even though we didn't have any of the life-saving, disease-eradicating drugs that society possesses now, somehow we seemed generally to be more healthy then. Yes, the newspapers carried stories about tuberculosis and polio outbreaks, and I can never forget the pall that settled on our avenue when an ambulance came to take away some poor youngster struck down by scarlet fever in the next street; but apart from little Davy and Grandpa Hyman I can't remember anybody else in the family, in the avenue or at school being felled by a dreadful disease. As for me, I understand that I had a bout of mastitis when I was not much more than a baby and I bear the scar of an operation for that on my neck today, but I can recall only two personal brushes with the medical profession, both when I was around eight.

The first was because of a large and painful whitlow – a virulent abscess – on my finger. Today it would have been swiftly dispersed by antibiotics; in 1937 I was offered two options: a surgical operation under local anaesthetic, or a more homeopathic but rather noisome remedy: several days with my finger wrapped in a bandage soaked in my own urine. After some swift soul-searching – who wants operations? – the Teslers chose the urine. Miraculously, it worked; but I wasn't very nice to be near for a few days.

I couldn't avoid a surgical operation with the second encounter. I can remember very clearly going up with my mother in a big red London bus to the Children's Hospital in Great Ormond Street for a consultation. The shelves in the specialist's consulting room were stacked with glass jars full of what looked to me like plums preserved in a light syrup. They were in fact tonsils; I had contracted a severe case of tonsillitis and it was agreed, though not necessarily by me, that my tonsils had to come out and join the rest of the specialist's specimens. I felt rather betrayed by my parents – I'd have preferred the tonsillitis – and I remember turning my back on them and my face to the wall when they visited me after I came out of the operation; but I was consoled by the fact that recuperating from tonsillectomy involved the consumption of a great deal of ice cream – almost the only thing you *could* consume after such an operation.

And it was here, as if in a dream, that I experienced *hot* ice cream. I woke up in the middle of one night to see a beautiful fairy with an ice cream tray slung from her neck, walking down the aisle between the rows of beds in the children's ward, like an usherette selling ice cream in a cinema, except that clouds of steam were emanating from the tray. "Hello, young man" said this angelic vision, "I've got some lovely hot ice cream here; would you like some?"

Dream or not, I wasn't going to pass up any of this, so I said "Yes please, miss." She handed me a tub and a little wooden spoon from the steaming tray, and it was pure ambrosia, food of the gods, the coolest, most soothing, most delicious ice cream I'd ever tasted; and then I went back to sleep.

My parents told me next day that I had imagined the whole thing. I hadn't, of course: the beautiful fairy had been some child's mother with a treat she was prepared to share with anybody else who happened to be awake, and the ice cream hadn't actually been hot: the steam was coming from the dry ice that kept it cold in its tray; but it was years before I accepted that reality and stopped asking for hot ice cream in ice cream parlours.

Inside No. 44

Upstairs at No.44 were two bedrooms, a bathroom, and a box-room. Our maid Winnie slept in the box-room, my parents in the front bedroom, my sister and I in our two little beds in the rear bedroom. The rear bedroom overlooked the garden and for most of the year and most of the time its position and its view were delightful. But I dreaded the long, sunny, beautiful summer evenings with the light pouring in through the curtain and the breathless hush outside. The hush was broken only by birdsong, the murmur of my parents and our neighbours and the sound of lawn-mowers from gardens up and down the avenue, but I had to get up to go to school in the morning for heaven's sake, and all this lyrical beauty was keeping me from my sleep.

Downstairs at No.44 was a hall, with a front room, a back room and a kitchen right at the end of it. The front room was for every day use, the back room was for special occasions. The front room had a dining table and chairs, a settee, the Sholem Aleichem bookcase, and a large dresser-like cabinet which housed among other things a state of the art gramophone and wireless. The back room had a deep-pile carpet, a great, voluminous leather sofa and matching arm-chairs, half a dozen occasional tables, a cocktail cabinet, another gramophone, various china ornaments and flower-vases: this was very much The Best Room, for entertaining.

And entertain they did, Dave and Stella. I remember the excitement and chatter and laughter of parties in that room, and I remember being part of the entertainment myself. As a toddler of two or three, although I couldn't read I could recognise our gramophone records by the shape and length of the titles on the labels, so the family party trick was to ask little butterball Brian to play this or that record, and off I would totter to the record pile, pick out the appropriate title, totter over to the gramophone and put it on the turntable. I was particularly good with records in Yiddish, my favourite (I liked the tune as well as the applause and laughter I received when I picked it out) being *Sha Sha Der Rabbi Geht* – Quiet! Quiet! The Rabbi's On His Way!

My other memory of The Best Room is associated with toothache. Whenever I was woken up by a painful tooth, my father would take me downstairs to the back room, open up the cocktail cabinet, soak a little piece of cotton-wool in some whisky and place it on whichever tooth was hurting. That would not only ease the pain but also, if I sucked hard enough on the whisky, would send me quickly back to sleep with a smile on my face. You would think that in later life I would either associate whisky with the pain and swear off it for ever or associate it with the relief from pain (and the smile on my face) and become addicted to it. Neither happened. I can take whisky or leave it. What a dull little fellow I turned out to be.

Disc Jockey Days

My affinity with gramophone records extended beyond *Sha Sha Der Rabbi Geht*. When I was small I had a little children's wind-up gramophone with very tinny sound reproduction which played 7-inch children's discs, of which my favourite was a medley of nursery rhymes including Patty-cake, Patty-cake, Baker's Man and Lazy Mary, Will You Get Up?, sung by a fruity, carefully enunciating baritone.

When I was older, I ransacked my parents' collection of gramophone records, leaving very much to one side the Yiddish ones, and played them on the machine in the front room cabinet, either emulating the BBC's first disc jockey Christopher Stone, as heard on the radio, or using some of them as sound effects and incidental music for little plays I'd make up from the comics I was reading. Not much more than ten years later I would be doing exactly the same thing at the British Forces Broadcasting Station in Trieste, except that the sound effects would be rather more professional and the radio documentaries or comedy programmes I had written would be considerably more elaborate; but I would still be spinning the discs myself.

I can remember the front-room cabinet's records to this day: the D'Oyly Carte Company and Selections from The Mikado; Bing Crosby and Brother Can You Spare A Dime?; Ambrose and his Orchestra and Tiger Rag, with vocal refrain by his drummer the Jewish comedian Max Bacon, who ended the record with the memorable line "Tiger! Schmiger! So long as you've got your health and strength, who needs Tigers?"; Sophie Tucker and My Yiddishe Momma (which Rosalind still remembers making her cry every time she heard it); the royal blue Decca labels with their gold lettering, the black and silver-labelled Brunswicks, the red and black Regal-Zonophones…

At the homes of the two Aunts and Uncles with whom the family visited most often in my pre-war childhood – Pearl and Sam (the Levingers) and Betty and Ben (the Fieldmans), more of whom later – there were plenty of cousins to play with but I used to make a bee-line at the Fieldmans' for Aunt Betty's books and at the Levingers' for Aunt Pearl's records. It was at Pearl's that I first encountered jazz on record, though I doubt if she, any more than I, knew that *jazz* was what it was.

It was in fact a Brunswick recording of the Boswell Sisters, the great 1920s close harmony trio, singing There'll Be Some Changes Made with the Dorsey Brothers Orchestra, and it was exhilarating and irresistible. As far as the world was concerned, this was just the popular music of the time; happily, the popular music of that time was infused with the heat and vigour and infectious syncopation of jazz, and it had me hooked for the rest of my life – as it did all the twentieth century's great popular songwriters, from George Gershwin and Irving Berlin to Jerome Kern and Cole Porter and onwards.

I did a good deal of singing and humming and whistling as a little lad. I liked the music I heard on the records and the radio, I could carry a tune, and I didn't hesitate to carry one at the drop of a hat, anywhere, any time. I won a fountain-pen for singing Cowboy at Markmanor Avenue's street party to celebrate the Coronation of Edward VIII in 1937, and I came first in a seaside children's talent competion in Southend with September In The Rain the same year. Both songs were published in 1937, received a great deal of radio air-play, which is where I heard them, and had their lyrics printed in McGlennon's Song Book, a sixpenny publication sold in Woolworth's which was devoted exclusively to the lyrics of the latest popular songs and which I couldn't wait to purchase every month. Both songs became standards, so I appear to have had a feeling for a good song even at the age of eight.

McGlennon's Song Book was still going strong in 1950 and I'm happy to say that, thirteen years after Michael Carr's and Al Dubin's lyrics for Cowboy and September In The Rain respectively were printed in its pulpy pages, so was a lyric of mine, The Girl Next Door, written in my first year at Oxford with music by Stanley Myers, Julian Dale and me. I've just re-read it, and it's quite dreadful; but look, this was over 50 years ago and the song was widely broadcast and recorded, notably by Ted Heath and his Orchestra, sung by Denis Lotis and Lita Roza. Blame it on my youth.

Reading

Reading books or comics at the meal table was quite properly not allowed at Markmanor Avenue. Like many other children before and after me, I soon exhausted the literary possibilities of the sauce bottle labels, though I must admit they gave me my introduction to the Houses of Parliament – so *that's* what HP stands for! – and what little I know of General Stonewall Jackson of the American Civil War, who according to the sauce originated the phrase OK. I couldn't wait to get down and get back to a book. As I've said, my bee-line at Aunt Betty's was straight to her bookshelves, and if I was still engrossed in one of her books when it was time for the family to go she would let me borrow it to finish at home. That's where I received my introduction to detective fiction, which is strange because you would have thought Betty's bookshelves would be filled with classics and romances. Perhaps that copy of John Dickson Carr's The Judas Window was Uncle Ben's. Whichever of them had bought it, I took it home and finished it next day and began a lifetime of reading crime and detective fiction for sheer unadulterated pleasure.

The Judas Window was published in 1938, so I was only about nine or ten by the time I got hold of it and my reading of crime and detection was considerably curtailed by the fact that, apart from Emil And The Detectives (which I didn't much like), Children's Libraries didn't contain a Crime And Detection section. I had to wait until I could join an Adult Library to further my addiction. Meanwhile, I fell back on my regular staple of Just William, Wurzel Gummidge, Biggles and Dr Doolittle, before I graduated to Jules Verne, Edgar Alan Poe (plenty of crime and detection there, of course) and historical adventure novels like The Three Musketeers, The Last Days Of Pompeii, Lorna Doone, In Old St Paul's and Ivanhoe. My son Simon, thirty years later, seemed to go straight from Tuffy The Tractor to James Bond; how times and cultures change.

And then there were the comic books. My first comics were Chick's Own and Tiger Tim's Weekly, everybody's starters, which used to break up the words beneath their pictures into sep-ar-ate syll-a-bles to make it easier for beginners to read. I moved on from those to Mickey Mouse Weekly – yes, I too was a member of The Mickey Mouse Club – and comic-strip comics like The Dandy and The

Beano and Film Fun; but my favourite British comics were those without any comic strips at all: The Hotspur, The Adventure, The Rover, The Wizard, all containing stirring stories of derring-do in the Empire, the first World War, the sports field and school. My memories of, I think it was The Hotspur's stories of action on the North-West Frontier of India, with a young British soldier (I can't remember his name) and a native side-kick armed with his favourite battle weapon "Clicky-Ba" (it was a cricket bat), inspired me to suggest twenty years or so later to my Head of Drama at ABC Television that we might do an action series about that period. Frontier was a great success, but alas it featured no Clickey-Ba.

While most of my comics were bought by my father, any pocket-money I had left after sweets, chocolate, ice-cream and McGlennon's Song Book was spent on comics too. But the best source for what was an incredible variety of good picture and story comics available to youngsters in those days was the door-step swap-shop. You'd take your bundle of comics, knock on the doors of the other boys in your street and see what they had to offer in exchange, the transactions taking place on the door-step while other members of the household tried to go in and out.

The door-step was where I encountered my first American comics, some time in 1937 when I was eight: a boy down the street had been given a whole bunch of these multicoloured delights by a recently arrived relative from the States. One of them was edition No.1 of Action Comics, containing the very first Superman strip. I got it in exchange for a Rover and two Wizards; I should have hung on to it. Interestingly, I heard on the radio the other day, in a news report of the re-launching of The Dandy, that The Dandy and The Beano also began publishing in 1937, so I must have had their earliest editions in my hands as well. All those early editions would be worth a good deal of money today: I should have hung on to the lot.

Stars Of Stage, Screen & Radio

Radio Fun was a strip comic from the same publishing stable as Film Fun. Both of them were printed in sooty black and white while all the others were wholly or partly in colour: even the story comics had riotously coloured covers illustrating one of the action adventures inside. Just as Film Fun was dedicated to comic-strips built round the popular film characters or performers of the day – its front page featured the escapades of Laurel and Hardy – so was Radio Fun full of strips about characters and performers from the BBC, and the adventures of "Big Hearted" Arthur Askey adorned its front page.

Radio was as big in those days as television is now, and the Teslers were dedicated radio-listeners. I was brought up on radio; not just the music programmes, the broadcasts by the great British dance bands of the day – Ambrose, Lew Stone, Carroll Gibbons and the others – but also the mystery serials and the comedy and variety shows. I still remember my first Paul Temple thriller with its sinister villain Tortoni, whose distorted voice was usually heard threatening Temple or his wife on the telephone, each week's episode introduced by the opening flourish of what I now know to be Fritz Kreisler's Humoresque but which then, played on the mouth-organ, seemed specially composed and particularly menacing.

Arthur Askey himself was the star of a bright and original comedy series called Bandwagon, with his sidekick Richard Murdoch. The series aired for the first time in 1938 and turned Arthur into one of the best-known and best-loved of all British entertainers. He had already made his name on the music halls and went on to become one of the first really big television stars of the early 1950s. He remained a star until he died in 1982, and twenty years after Bandwagon I was producing him in his own television series for ATV.

There were many other radio comedy shows, whose titles I can't recall until we get to the war years when radio, and particularly radio comedy, helped to sustain the Teslers and the rest of the nation through some pretty tough times. But I certainly remember the names of the pre-war comedians, perhaps because they were also spot-lit from time to time in radio variety shows like Music Hall (whose signature tune is running through my head as I type these words) – the magnificent Billy Bennett ("Almost A Gentleman"), Gillie Potter ("speaking to you from England"), the gormless innocent Stainless Stephen (a staple of Radio Fun), Sandy Powell as an hilariously awful ventriloquist, Will Hay, Max Miller, Robb Wilton, Stanley Holloway with his great Yorkshire comic monologues… Many of them had professional careers as long-lived as Arthur Askey's, going on through and beyond the 1939-45 war. Stanley Holloway ultimately went from music hall to musical theatre as one of the Broadway, West End and Hollywood stars of My Fair Lady; he made his last film, Journey Into Fear, in 1975 at the age of 85, seven years before he died. Tough old birds, those music hall artists.

One of the radio shows that made a great impression on the British public, including me, was an entertainment magazine at eight o'clock on Monday night called, fairly naturally, Monday Night At Eight. It was a mixture of songs and sketches – including a weekly crime and detection story called Inspector Hornleigh Investigates and a series of twist-in-the-tail playlets featuring your friendly local dustman, Syd – together with a puzzle or two in Puzzle Corner and a quiz. Presented and co-produced by a bright young man called Ronnie Waldman, it was hugely popular. I can still sing you the signature tune for the friendly dustman spot – "Day after day, I'm on my way, Singing Rags, Bottles and Bones…"and the opening and closing themes of the programme itself, opening with "It's Monday night at eight o'clock, Now can't you hear the chimes?.." and ending with "It's Monday Night at nine o'clock, It's time to say good night…" The programme began in 1938. Fourteen years later, in 1952, Ronnie Waldman was Head of Light Entertainment at BBC Television's Lime Grove Studios, and I was working for him – my first boss – as a very young trainee television producer.

Movies

Both my parents loved the movies and, while Winnie looked after Rosalind and until I was old enough to go by myself, they used to take me with them for their regular Saturday afternoon treat at the local cinema. For years afterwards I thought that Saturday afternoon was the only time to go to the movies: any other time just didn't feel right. The two local cinemas I best remember were the Savoy, Leyton, a ten-minute walk from Markmanor Avenue, and the Granada in Hoe Street, Walthamstow, a five-minute walk and a trolley-bus ride away, but there were several other cinemas in the area, both regular and "flea-pit", and we happily patronised them all.

My memories of the films I saw in the thirties, with or without my parents, and of the whole experience of film-going in those days, are remarkably clear. All cinemas except those in the West End featured continuous performances, so once you were inside you didn't have to leave until the lights went up and the projectionist went home. And they were long performances, too. Today, you see a film, some commercials and a batch of trailers for forthcoming attractions. In those days, in addition to a trailer for the next attraction, you saw the big film, a supporting picture (the B Movie), a newsreel, a cartoon and an additional short subject – a comedy with Leon Errol or Robert Benchley or a documentary feature like Pathe Pictorial or Look At Life, often one of each.

In the afternoon and evening performances between the movies, a massive, glittering cinema organ would rise from the orchestra pit, sumptuously lit with rose and gold spotlights, the white-tuxedoed organist playing a medley of popular songs and light classics while the screen shimmered and glowed with a slide-show of changing colours and patterns. Since the performances were continuous, you could pop into the cinema whenever it suited you; the only problem was that if you popped in after the big film had started you had to sit through the entire programme, organ interval and all, before you could find out what had happened at its beginning – but then you usually stayed to see the rest of the film over again anyway.

A child could see a U Certificate film (U for Universal) unaccompanied; for an A Certificate (A, appropriately enough, for Adult), you had to be accompanied by an adult. Any adult. So you went along to the cinema, trotted up to some strange man in the queue (there never seemed to be a single, matronly woman queuing for the pictures), proffered your sixpence for the ticket and asked "Can you take me in, please Mister?" Once you were inside the auditorium you both went your separate ways.

Think of the risks involved in that process, let alone in the getting to and from the cinema. Like my contemporaries all over the U.K. I was cheerfully going to the pictures by myself from the age of nine. After school and tea on a Friday afternoon, I would walk down Markmanor Avenue, across Bridge Road, down Blyth Road (a dark and gloomy thoroughfare I still dream about) into Leabridge Road, catch a trolley-bus to the Granada Walthamstow, accost some stranger in the queue – "Can you take me in, Mister?" – and then re-trace my journey home after the film in an early evening already dark in the winter months, a small, solitary, vulnerable child; can you imagine doing that today?

The movies I remember are an extraordinarily varied collection: thrillers, comedies, dramas, musicals, the occasional children's film. Whatever my parents wanted to see, I saw, and their tastes were wide-ranging – or rather, as with so many other cinema-goers, theirs was a cinema-going *habit*: they saw whatever was showing at the local cinema; and so did I – twice weekly if the movies changed mid-week as they did in some of the locals. You didn't necessarily go to see a particular film: you just went to the pictures. And though you might see a few stinkers as a result, particularly in the B movie department, the overall standard was pretty good. Certainly the movies I remember enjoying as a lad between the ages of five and ten, from 1935 to 1939, stand up very well. If I saw them in the years in which they were released I must have been a pretty precocious cinema-goer, but I know I saw them all for the first time before the war.

The earliest films I remember, Leslie Howard in The Scarlet Pimpernel and Gracie Fields in Sing As We Go, were released in 1934 when I was five; my memories of Fred Astaire and Ginger Rogers in Top Hat and Robert Donat and Madeleine Carroll in Hitchcock's The Thirty-Nine Steps, both films released in 1935, are very clear (and I've loved musicals and thrillers ever since). I remember coming out of the cinema stunned by Things To Come (1936); I remember laughing my head off at Will Hay in Oh Mr Porter (1937) and loving Snow White And

The Seven Dwarfs in the same year (we missed its beginning at the Savoy, Leyton, coming in as the Dwarfs were marching home from work – "Heigh Ho! Heigh Ho! As home from work we go!"– so we had to sit through the whole programme again to get the story straight). I particularly remember being taken by my mother to see a melodrama called Woman Chases Man (1937) when we were on a seaside holiday (presumably Dad was looking after Rosalind), which sticks in my mind because my mother wept during a scene in which Miriam Hopkins sat at the hospital bedside of Joel McCrae, who was in an oxygen tent dangerously ill with pneumonia; I now realise she was weeping because her father had died in exactly that way the previous year.

I remember the remarkable voice and breezy cheekiness of Gracie Fields and the gormless good humour of George Formby, the two great Lancashire music hall stars, who each seemed to make at least one comedy a year in the thirties (twenty years or so later, I would be producing both of them in television shows for ITV). I remember being bowled over by the charm and wit of Cary Grant in Topper (1937) and the thrills of Hitchcock's The Lady Vanishes (1938). I remember the excitement of spectacular action-adventure films like Too Hot To Handle (Clark Gable and Walter Pidgeon as rival newsreel cameramen) and Test Pilot (Clark Gable and Spencer Tracy as rival air aces), both in 1938. I remember being enchanted by the marvellous Wizard Of Oz in 1939 and trying to sing its songs as we came away from the cinema.

I've seen most if not all of those films again since and, as I say, they stand up pretty well. Except...When television began to bite into their audiences in the 1950s, the cinema exhibitors set up the Film Industry Defence Organisation – FIDO – to pay UK film producers and distributors not to sell films to their deadly rival. In the middle of the 1960s, when I was Director of Programmes at ABC Television, FIDO collapsed, and a growing flood of movies became available to the television companies. I couldn't wait to run through my first package of MGM titles, all those great films that I had loved throughout the thirties and forties: a film-buff's dream come true. And for the most part they were still great: the dialogue still punchy, the characterisation still vivid, the music still compelling; but oh, the special effects!

Movie-making had moved on dazzlingly fast since the thirties; new technology had accustomed us to a far higher level of realism in the cinema, and all those stunning action sequences in Too Hot To Handle and Test Pilot and films like them were now only too obviously back-projected. That wasn't Clark Gable in a fragile bi-plane risking his life to shoot newsreel footage of a fire on board a battleship, ammunition exploding all around him: that was Clark Gable sitting in a studio mock-up of an airplane cockpit in front of a large back-projection screen. Yes, I know he wouldn't actually have been flying over an exploding battleship in the 1960s either, but state-of-the-art special effects would have persuaded you that he was. And today they would put you in the cockpit, flying the plane yourself.

Music Hall

Music Hall and variety were my father's particular joys and some of my happiest times as a growing lad were spent with him and my mother at three great variety theatres: the Hackney Empire, the nearest for Walthamstow dwellers; the London Palladium in the West End, for special treats; and the Holborn Empire, geographically in between. At the Palladium and the two Empires we saw all the great artistes of the music hall era – including most of those noted above – before television first fed it with new stars and then killed it off. I particularly remember Max Miller at the Holborn Empire, a favourite venue of his; and going on the complicated journey by trolley-bus and bus to the London Palladium to see lavish musical revues starring Tommy Trinder or Flanagan and Allen and the rest of what was to become known as the Crazy Gang.

These revues were my first experience of the thrill of a big orchestra accompanying lines of dancing girls in glamorous production numbers, and I never forgot that thrill. Fourteen years or so later, with BBC Television, I would be directing big production numbers with lines of glamorous dancing girls like these. And a few years later still, I would be producing television shows in that same Hackney Empire, by then converted into a television studio, and a weekly television variety show on Sunday night from the London Palladium itself, with a line-up of Tiller Girl dancers who could have been the grand-daughters of the Tiller Girls I saw in those shows before the war.

All these echoes of the future, of music and movies and radio and music-hall… In Wordsworth's Ode, Intimation Of Immortality, "Shades of the prison-house begin to close Upon the growing boy". In my case, happily, the shades appear to have been those of show business.

Something's Coming...

Moving Upward – And Outward

By the middle of the thirties, all the Hyman girls had married and moved out of the East End. Annie, married long before the others in 1919, had relocated to Stamford Hill with her husband Harry Kaiser, a gentle, good-natured tailor's cutter, and their son Willie, born in 1920. Pearl must have married Sam Levinger around the time of Stella and Dave's wedding, since their elder daughter, Irene, was the same age as me; Sam was a taxi-driver but he came from what appears to have been quite a wealthy family and he and Pearl, together with Irene and their younger daughter Hilary, born two years later, moved into the family's large Victorian house in Clapton, which in due course they inherited.

Betty married Ben Fieldman in 1932: a particularly good match, the other Hyman girls thought, because Ben shared a prosperous business with his brother, manufacturing mantles and ladies coats and selling them in their West End shop. After they married, Betty and Ben moved to a fashionable house in Finchley. Denise tells me I was a page boy at the wedding. I don't remember it, and Betty seems not to have wanted it: a little three-year old boy in his velvet suit was either going to steal a wedding or ruin it, but big sister Stella appears to have insisted. Denise was born in 1935; Nigel and Lindsay were post-war babies, arriving in 1946 and 1949 respectively.

In 1935, Eve, the last of the Hyman girls, married Mick Chason, a cheerful, good-looking young man of whom everyone was fond, and I do remember being enthusiastically employed as a page-boy at that wedding; at six, after all, I was hardly going to steal the show, no matter how resplendent my new, blue velvet suit might have been, and I was old enough not to make a mess of anything I was asked to do. Like Pearl and Sam, after they were married Eve and Mick moved to Clapton, though to a fairly humble flat; he was a hard-working travelling salesman in cleaning materials for Ibbetsons at the time, but his diligence and charm in due course won him the position of Sales Director for Jeyes, and a nice house in Southgate.

The Chasons' first son, Derek, came along two years later (their second, Andrew, not until 1944); and though I was perfectly happy playing with my girl cousins at family get-togethers – Willie was far too old for us and we saw comparatively little of him – I was glad to have another young male in the family and spent a great deal of time with little Derek in his early years, mostly trying to make him laugh. Interestingly un-Jewish, even exotic names the four younger sisters chose for their children: Denise, Nigel, Lindsey, Irene, Hilary, Derek, Andrew, Rosalind (whose middle name is Bernice); I have no middle name, but the name I do possess does at least look exotic on my birth certificate, where Bryan is spelled with a 'y'. Perhaps Betty wasn't the sole romantic among the Hyman girls.

The Hyman home was therefore empty of all its children by 1935 when Harris died, and it made sense for Yetta to sell the house in Globe Road and the bakery business, and with the proceeds to move near one of her daughters. She chose Markmanor Avenue, and bought No.13, a little house at the bottom of our street, past which I used to walk every day on my way to school.

Meanwhile, among the brothers-in-law Dave seemed to be doing increasingly well. By now, he had set up his own millinery business with a partner named William – "Bill" – Fish, and Tesler & Fish had got off to a good start. I remember Mr Fish well. He was a large man, built very much on the lines of Oliver Hardy, and I have a vivid mental picture of him on a hot summer's day, walking up Markmanor Avenue to our house in his blue serge suit, bowler hat on his head, mopping the perspiration from his face with a large coloured handkerchief, on his way to a business discussion with my father, with me breaking off from a wrestling bout on the pavement with another Jackie, Jackie Smith, to say "Hello, Mr Fish" as he passed by.

And of course, as the photographs have already shown, we were well enough off to have a maid: Winnie, the pretty little girl from Wales, whose principal job was to help my mother look after Rosalind, lend a hand with the cleaning and shopping and, as I clearly remember, serve tea when we had visitors, dressed like a Lyons Tea House Nippie in that little black dress, white cap and apron.

Holidays

A pretty reliable guide as to how well my father's business was doing was our annual trip to the seaside. My earliest summer holiday recollections are of train rides to what I now know was Southend Station, followed by taxi rides to a boarding house in the hinterland of Southend itself. I don't recall the name of the road, but

I still remember the smell of frying bacon that wafted toward us as the taxi approached our very non-Jewish boarding house.

My mother, while not devoutly Orthodox herself, kept a vaguely Orthodox home in which the Sabbath candle was lit on Friday night with the appropriate blessing and some of the more easily observed dietary laws were maintained, including the strict avoidance of pork in all its forms. The trouble was that my parents both loved bacon, so though it was never allowed in No.44 Markmanor Avenue, they cheerfully dug into it on holiday in our Gentile boarding houses; and so, very gladly, did I.

Southend was the natural holiday destination for East Londoners: an easy train journey east to the coast of Essex, a jolly cockles-and-winkles kind of resort with decent beaches, a large Fun Fair and a magnificent pier. The pier was over a mile long and is still to this day the longest in the world, with a concert-party theatre at the end of it and a little train to take you all the way there if you didn't feel up to a long and bracing walk. It was an ideal day's outing for the fashionable young East Enders of the time when Dave and Stella were in their early twenties – those strolls along the promenade where they probably first caught sight of each other. But now, married and with a couple of children, it was the destination for our annual family holiday – the traditional last week in July, first week in August – and this time nowhere near the promenade: our first boarding houses were a long bus journey away from the beach.

As my father's business prospects improved, however, we began the progression first to boarding houses nearer the sea, so that we had a long walk rather than a long bus ride to the beach; then to Westcliff, the comparatively smart other half of Southend; then to small private hotels in the rather smarter Essex resort of Margate, on the southern side of the Thames estuary; then to Margate's more sophisticated other half, Cliftonville, and hotels nearer to the beach; then all the way south and west to Boscombe in Dorsetshire and finally to its grander neighbour Bournemouth, this time and at last to large, luxurious Jewish hotels on the promenade itself. Goodbye bacon; hello salt beef and chopped liver. You could plot the progress on a graph: the further south, the nearer to the beach, the steeper the gradient from boarding house to private hotel to big family hotel, the better Tesler & Fish were doing.

The family photographs monitor the progress from shingly beaches to golden sands; and my memory of those summer holidays is a great warm blur of deckchairs and sand-castles, of long walks back to the boarding houses of Southend or long climbs up the zig-zag paths of the cliffs of Cliftonville; of playing in the sand and in the sea with my sister; of Rossi's delicious soft twirly vanilla ice cream; of train rides to the end of Southend pier to see the concert-parties – oh, how I used to adore those end-of-pier shows; of the Punch And Judy and children's talent shows on the beaches; of parades with bands and floats and flowers along the promenades; of being photographed on the beach sitting on Margate's scarily realistic stuffed tiger or taking part in sandcastle competitions with Teddy Tail of the Daily Mail; of my father trying to teach me to swim by supporting me horizontally in the sea and my sinking like a stone whenever he let go; of long walks along the promenade with Dad telling me to take deep breaths of the salt sea air because it would do me so much good. Seventy years later, I'm still taking long walks and deep breaths, wherever and whenever I can.

There's a fascinating pair of pictures in the album of my father and me, taken about ten years apart, standing side by side on exactly the same stretch of stone steps leading down to the beach at Cliftonville, almost certainly taken by the same beach photographer, whose pitch this would have been. I'm six or seven years old in the first, holding my father's hand, and something like sixteen in the second, with my arm round his shoulder. In the first, my father is a trim, slim, good looking young man in his mid-thirties, wearing a short-sleeved sports shirt; in the second, he's still good-looking but now he's in his mid-forties, a little portly, a successful business man in a business suit and collar and tie. But can this nice, open-faced little boy in the first picture be the cocky, self-satisfied, patronising teenager in the second? I'm afraid so. However, my arrogance didn't stop me from holidaying with my parents and sister, which I continued to do right up to my early twenties: we were all staying together in a Bournemouth hotel in 1950 when my friends in Oxford telephoned to say I'd got my degree.

Back To The East End

Winnie didn't accompany us on our holidays: she went back to Wales to her own family for the annual fortnight; but the family photographs show that from time to time, at least in the early years, Big Booba and Zaida – my paternal grand-parents Sophie and Gershon – did come with us. I haven't the faintest idea how they felt about the bacon.

At some time in the early thirties, perhaps when Stella and Dave set up home in Markmanor Avenue, my father rented a flat for my grandparents in a tenement block in Whitechapel: Brady Street Buildings. Brady Street is off Whitechapel Road just after it has taken over from the Mile End Road as one of the great thoroughfares cutting through the heart of the East End. Brady Street Buildings was a large tenement complex with iron fire-escapes on the exteriors of multi-storied blocks built on three sides of a tarmac-covered courtyard. When they weren't calling to – or shouting at – each other across it, the residents used the courtyard as a concourse. Their kids used it as a playground and tradesmen used it as the base from which to sell their wares. In Brady Street, just as in the period movies of New York's Lower East Side, the tradesmen yelled up to the residents with their wares and the residents yelled down to the tradesmen with their orders, lowered ropes and little baskets with money in them and hauled up the daily beigels and chollah, eggs and milk and fruit and vegetables.

Booba and Zaida's flat had a sitting room, a bedroom, a kitchen and a bathroom, and we used to visit them for lunch on Sundays. The four of us would travel by bus and tram from Walthamstow, through Clapton and Dalston and Hackney, coming out at the T-junction at the end of Cambridge Heath Road where Mile End Road became Whitechapel Road; and there, a little way down on the right, was Brady Street. Cross Whitechapel Road, stop at the corner shop to buy some comics, turn into Brady Street, past the gent's hairdressers, past the sweetshop, into the Buildings, climb up the stairs – three flights of them – and there's the flat, with its warm smells of furniture polish, Zaida's pipe tobacco and Booba's delicious, waist-busting Sunday lunch.

After lunch, Dave and Stella would go off to a movie or a matinee performance at the nearby Grand Palais Yiddish theatre or just go into the bedroom for a post-prandial snooze, and Rosalind and I would look at our comics or draw, or have sword-fights with weapons cut out of the cardboard stiffeners that came back with Zaida's shirts from the laundry, while Zaida smoked his pipe or dozed by the electric fire and Booba prepared tea.

But sometimes we'd get to Brady Street early, postpone lunch and all go off to 'The Lane', to enjoy the noisy bustle of the crowds and street-traders and perhaps do a little shopping – usually, if my father had his way, for what my mother called *shmochnehs*, Yiddish for rubbishy gimmicks, which my father could never resist and was always bringing home on his way back from work or a walk. The Lane, referred to as Petticoat Lane because part of it ran along the East side of Petticoat Square, occupied most of the T- junction formed by Middlesex Street and Wentworth Street in Aldgate and was a short tram-ride from Brady Street along Whitechapel Road. It was the biggest street market in the East End of London and one of the city's most colourful sights, thronging with visitors, overflowing with market stalls of every kind, bursting with racks of clothes, stacks of bird and pet cages, lines of toy stalls, food stalls, confectionery stalls, drink stalls, with street-traders shouting their wares, shoppers haggling over prices, street auctioneers

Stella and Dave.

Stella's parents: Harris and Yetta Hyman. Here, Yetta poses with her first grandson, Annie's son Willie. Yetta is always known to me as Little Booba.

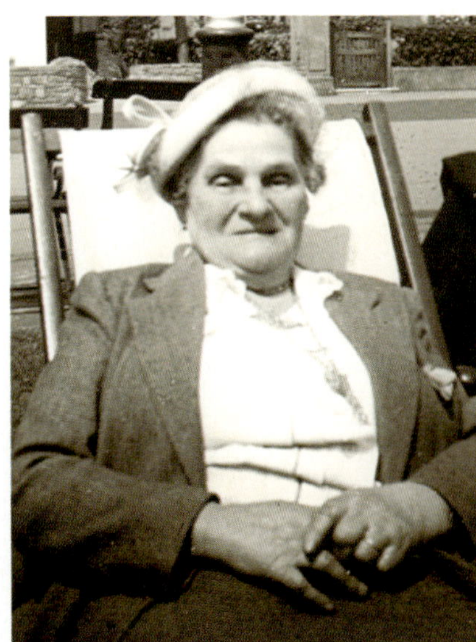

Dave's parents: Gershon and Sophie Tesler, in Russia...

... and in England *(below)*, where in time they become, to me, 'Big Booba' and 'Zaida'.

Dave, as a Russian teenager *(left)*, and as the English Young Sport *(below)*.

Stella, the fashionable young Jewish princess – one of five.

Young men on the promenade, Dave second from the left; and also playing around on the beach *(right)*. On another promenade, a group of young women, with Stella in the middle of the line.

It isn't too long before these two young people catch each other's eye. It's just possible to make out the words "I Love You" on the piece of paper Dave is holding up for the camera...

12 June 1927: Dave and Stella marry. Eve, Pearl and Betty act as bridesmaids.

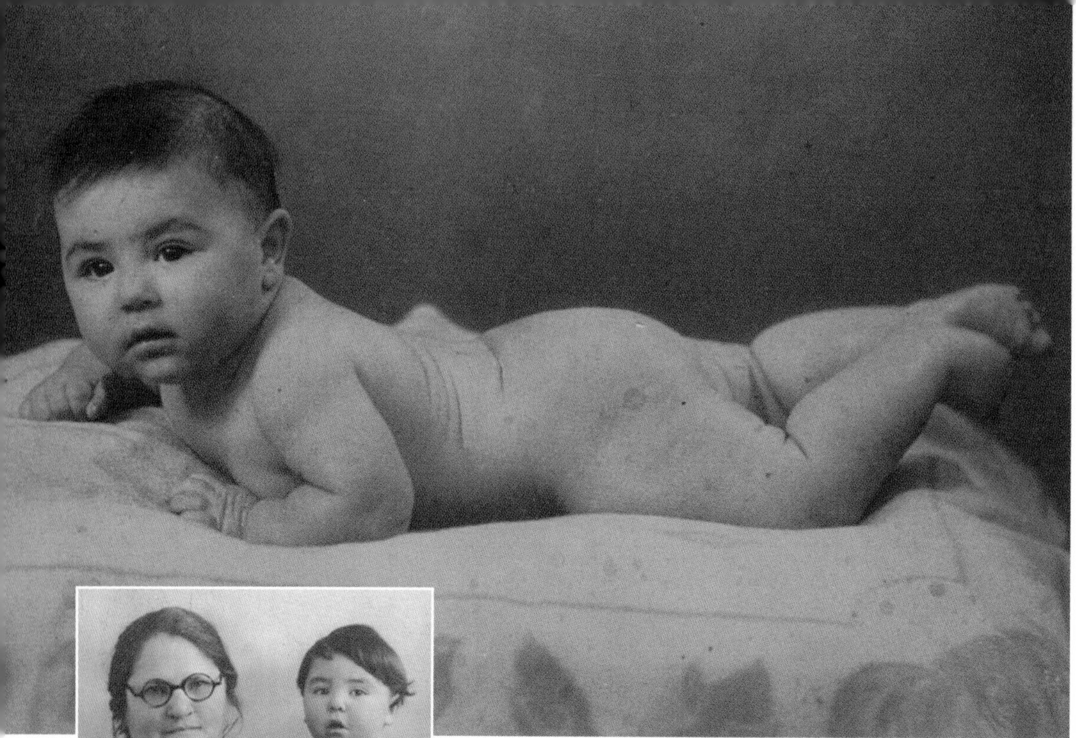

Born beautiful on 19 February 1929, I rapidly become a pudding that only a Booba could love...

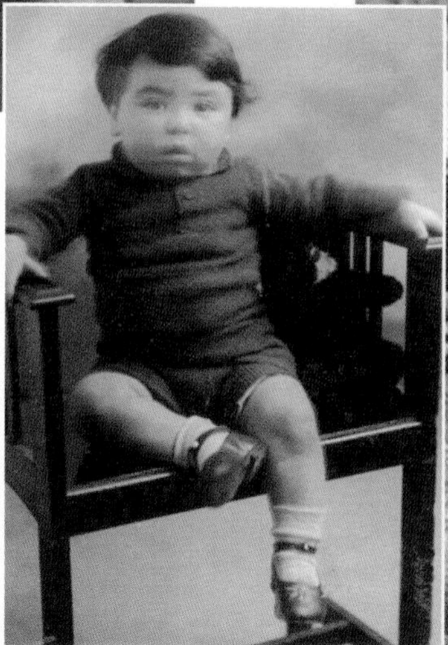

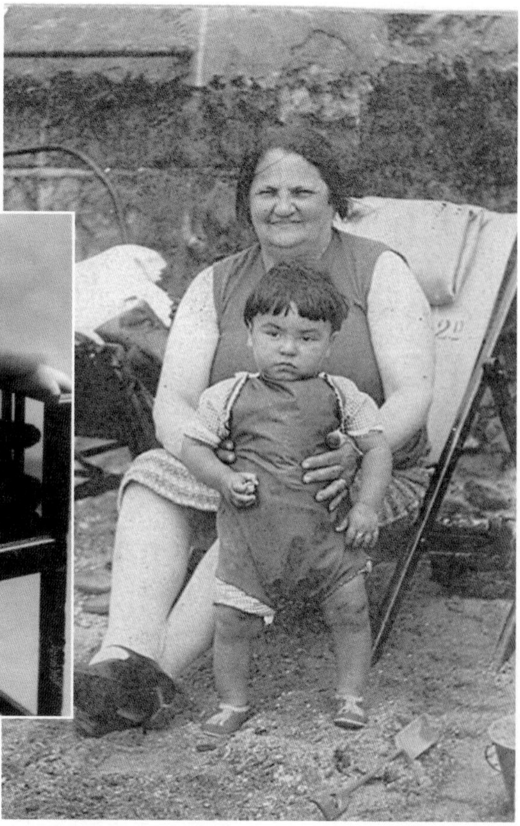

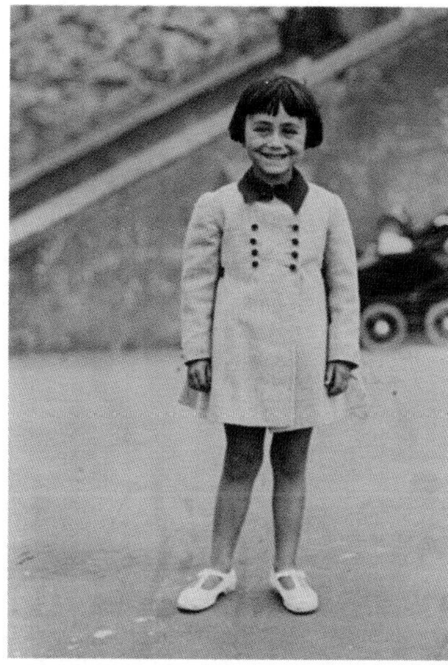

...whereas Rosalind Bernice, born beautiful on 5 April 1933, stays beautiful.

Family and holiday life for the young Tesler family.

... with Zaida at Margate *(below)*...

...with Teddy Tail from the Daily Mail *(above)*

Winnie, our Welsh maid, above with me in the garden, and left with Rosalind outside No 44 Markmanor Avenue.

Stella's siblings and their wedding days: brother Alf, with his wife Sophie *(left)*; sister Pearl, with her husband Sam *(below)*; sister Eve with husband Mick *(bottom left)* and sister Betty with husband Ben *(bottom right)*.

Can the nice open-faced little boy on the left really have become the cocky self-satisfied teenager below?

The Boxing Years - Barry Levison is my opponent, with Jack Greenstock as referee; and *(right)* walking with Dad on Richmond Bridge.

Top: Sybourn Street Elementary School, class of 1937. I am sitting in the centre of the front row, with Harold Eckert on the extreme left, and Jackie Shafron on my immediate left. Tony Manzi is at the end of the row. Phillie Solomons is third from the left in the third row; Louis Edmonds at the left in the back row. *Above:* Chiswick County School for Boys' school play in 1944 - JB Priestley's Desert Highway. I am second left, with Norman Millar on right.

Hounslow Barracks 1947: the end of basic training. Private Tesler is third from left, back row.

Woolwich Arsenal Depot 1948: now Gunner Tesler and an army-trained clerk. Adrian Brown and I are second and third from right, back row. *Right:* on the steps of the station control room in Trieste.

Above: in civvies in Trieste, with John Jacobs, Johnny Rothwell and two local girls. *Right:* with Richard Hancock, John Jacobs and station mascot Boma. *Below:* producing a weekly general knowledge quiz. Station staff (John Jacobs, Johnny Rothwell, Peter Hunt and Ted Moulding) against a military police team, with quiz master Jimmy Brown.

calling punters into their non-stop shop-front auctions.

For the youngest Teslers it was the world's biggest sweet shop, in which my own favourite indulgences were halva, the sesame sweetmeat for which I still salivate, and great, jagged chunks, as transparent as ice-cubes, of what could only have been pure, solid sugar. I haven't seen that delicacy since those pre-war days: it's probably been banned. The Lane is still among the East End's biggest and best known attractions, and it's even more colourful today, but vastly different culturally: the immigrants who populate this part of the city are now mostly from the Indian sub-continent; the colourfulness now is Oriental.

Another great treat for me on those Brady Street afternoons was a visit with my father to the Devonshire Sporting Club. This was a venue for boxing matches in the Whitechapel Road run by a boxing promoter named Jack Solomons; its club status gave it both a little tone – the spectators sat in plush tiered seats on all sides of the boxing ring – and a licence, not only to promote boxing matches on Sunday afternoons but also to sell liquor to the club members who paid to see them. I acquired a taste for boxing from those afternoons with my father at the Devonshire but not, I'm glad to say, for liquor.

Dad was a real fight fan. He was a pretty feisty little fellow himself: I guess you had to be, to look after yourself in the East End in the early years of the last century. I have one particular memory of a celebratory dance after a wedding or a barmitzvah. I was, I suppose, four or five years old and, like the other little kids who drive you mad on such occasions, excitedly weaving in and out of the dancers and chasing each other round the floor, I got under the feet of one brawny couple and was pushed rather forcefully out of the way and sworn at by the male dancer. Dad was also on the floor at the time, saw what happened, confronted the fellow and invited him to apologise or come outside to discuss it rather more freely. The fellow apologised. I have another memory of that evening. I was obviously rather generally over-excited – perhaps I'd been given a few sips of wine – and as we arrived at our destination in the taxi that brought us home from the do I threw up. My father gave the taxi driver an extra couple of quid to make up for the mess.

Boxing was one of the few opportunities available to the unemployed young men of the East End to better themselves after the Depression years of the late '20s and early '30s. They literally fought their way out of the slums, and venues like the Devonshire Sporting Club gave them the chance to do so. I saw some superb fights there with great young boxers of the thirties, several of whom went on to become English and Empire champions, like Eric Boon and Arthur Danahar. Some of them, like Peter Kane, even went on to be World Champions; and some, like Alby Day or Harry Mizler or Kid Silver – extraordinary how these names have stuck in my memory – simply gave the spectators a good show, always fighting their heart out, to the roars of fight fans like my father – "Get inside!" – "Kill him!" – "Murder him!"

The Devonshire was a fairly regular Sunday treat, but I also remember one particular afternoon when my father took me to The Ring at Blackfriars, a world-famous open-air boxing stadium, long since vanished. This must have been some sort of special occasion because Blackfriars is a considerable distance from Brady Street – perhaps we went there by Underground from Aldgate East station; but I remember it was a brilliantly sunny day, and the stadium was packed and heaving with excitement and anticipation: in my recollection it's like one of those flickering black and white cinema newsreels of American open-air championship fights in the teens and twenties of the last century – like Jack Johnson versus Jess Willard or Jack Dempsey versus Gene Tunney – sequences that television likes to run in sports documentaries.

I've no idea who was fighting on this occasion, but I do remember two especially desirable signatures I managed to get for my autograph book: Ted 'Kid' Lewis, who had been a highly respected world champion, and Tom Mix, an American cowboy movie star over here for a publicity tour, who rode his horse into the stadium down the aisle through the spectators to the ring, and vaulted over the ropes from his saddle to be introduced to the crowd.

My father used to stay up all night to hear the radio commentaries on the Big Fights taking place in the United States, just as my future wife's father used to stay up to listen to the Test Cricket commentaries from Australia. When I was sixteen, my father arranged for an old friend of his, Jack Greenstock, a previous contender for the British middleweight title, to give me and my friend Barry Levison weekly boxing lessons. Fired by my father's enthusiasm and Jack Greenstock's training expertise, I rather took to the sport. I founded my Secondary School's Boxing Club, and carried on boxing in the early months of my two years of National Service. I was a Gunner – a Private – in the Royal Artillery, stationed in Rhyl in North Wales, and entered the Army's North-West Command Novices Championships. I won my first fight, enjoyed a walkover to the second round because my opponent scratched, and found myself in the Finals of my weight division.

Needless to say, I invited my mother and father and Rosalind to Rhyl to watch the contest. My opponent and I might well have weighed the same, but I was comparatively small and stocky and he was tall and slim, and that meant he had a very much longer reach than I. I tried to get inside and under it, to hammer at his midriff, but I simply couldn't get past his straight left and the effort rapidly tired me, so I was getting clobbered.

What made it worse was that I was aware through the roar of the crowd that my father the fight fan, completely caught up in the fury and excitement of the battle, was yelling instructions to both contestants as he always used to do at the fights – "Get inside!", "Kill him!", "Murder him!". "Get inside!" was for me; I'm afraid "Kill him!" and "Murder him!" were for the other fellow; and he very nearly did. The next day my face was bruised and swollen and my right eye was a study in black, blue and yellow, but my father was proud of me: I'd still been upright at the end of the bout; in spite of all that punishment I hadn't gone down.

Rumours Of War

My walks with my father weren't limited to summer holiday promenades along the sea front. We had always gone for walks together, practically from the day I first managed to stand and put one foot in front of the other, and we continued to do so well into my late teens: there's a nice picture of the two of us on a Sunday morning stroll across Richmond Bridge in which I look about eighteen, so it must have been taken just before I went into the Army.

The walks I look back on with the greatest affection are the winter ones, when I was a very small boy and used to put my hand in my father's coat pocket for extra warmth, sometimes actually inside his glove alongside his own hand, as we walked along while he told me stories of woodcutters and wolves and magic woods which I now realise were old Russian folk tales that his father must have told him when he was a little boy in Baremel'. In the later thirties, when I was around nine or ten, we had got into the habit of taking regular early evening strolls at weekends in the spring and summer, when I didn't have to get up early the next morning for school. Away we'd go, along Markmanor Avenue and the surrounding streets, enjoying the air and exercise, chatting and laughing with our neighbours and friends, all of us relaxed and comfortable and at ease.

In the spring of 1939, however, the atmosphere was very different. Those early evening walks were now sombre and subdued; the groups of neighbours gathered at their garden gates in the dusk spoke in hushed voices, their faces serious and concerned, their mood foreboding. The conversation now was about the situation in Europe and the growing menace of Hitler and Nazi Germany; the talk was of war. Fiercely patriotic, my father applied for Naturalization: he'd lived in Britain for more than twenty years; he felt British; he certainly sounded British – unlike his own father and many of his friends he had no trace of a foreign accent – and if there was to be a war he wanted to demonstrate his gratitude to the country that had given him the opportunity to succeed by formally becoming a British citizen. He swore his Oath of Allegiance on 7 June 1939.

Certainly, through those spring months and the early summer of 1939, war between Britain and Germany seemed inevitable, and Londoners didn't need the gloomy prophecies of the newspapers to believe that, if it came, London would be the immediate and principal target.

The cinemas had re-released the H.G. Welles film Things To Come, the opening sequence of which seemed an ominously prophetic vision of what now threatened the capital. In it, war erupts between Britain and an unnamed enemy and the enemy's bombers descend on London in their hundreds, disregarding the searchlights and the anti-aircraft guns, raining their bombs down onto an exposed and helpless city; buses and taxis collide with each other under the bright lights of the West End and there is panic in the streets as familiar landmarks explode and collapse and go up in flames – Nelson's Column, Westminster Abbey, the Houses of Parliament. I last saw this movie seventy years ago but its images are still imprinted on my brain. It's what everybody then believed: the bomber would always get through; and we had seen in the newsreels of the Spanish Civil War how devastatingly effective the bombers of the Nazi airforce, the Luftwaffe, could be when they did get through. Clearly, while striving for peace through negotiation, the country had to prepare itself for war and especially for war from the air.

Preparing For Doomsday

The common fear was that the Germans would use poison gas in their bombs as well as high explosive, just as they had done in the trench warfare of the First World War. To protect the people from this, the Government began to issue rubber gas-masks to everybody – adults, children, even babies: ugly pieces of equipment with great pig-like snouts to filter the air that we would breathe during an attack. We were supposed to carry them slung over our shoulders wherever we went, in cardboard boxes supplied by the Government with carrying-straps of string.

Enterprising marketeers soon started to sell cute little covers for the cardboard boxes made up of all kinds of material, with carrying-straps to match. That was the only thing that was ever cute about the whole business: the masks themselves made us look like monsters from some grotesque science-fiction movie, and I can still remember the ghastly smell of their rubber and the little farting noise they made as you breathed in and out.

Up until now, the tranquil peace and quiet of Markmanor Avenue had been disturbed only by the tricycle bells of icecream vendors in their smart uniforms and peaked caps, pedalling slowly down the street at weekends with gaily decorated freezer cabinets in front of their handlebars, crying "Stop me and buy one!" – and we'd rush out with our pennies to do just that. My favourites were the Walls' Sno-frutes, coloured sticks of fruit-flavoured ice, triangular in shape like Toblerone bars.

I don't know where the Sno-frute vendors went on weekdays: the weekday pitch outside our school was taken up by the Eldorado tricycle, dispensing slim slabs of delicious vanilla or strawberry icecream: penny a slab, ha'penny for a half, sliced on the diagonal.

But now the street was rumbling and clattering with the noise of lorries bringing Anderson Shelters – small Nissen huts made of galvanised steel – to our houses, and council workmen installing them three feet deep in our back gardens and covering them with earth. These little bomb shelters, named after the Home Secretary of the day, were designed to protect Londoners from pretty well anything but a direct hit, and in due course London was to be very thankful for them. They did however spoil the lawn and line of a well-kept garden, and my father persuaded the authorities that we didn't need one at No 44 because the family would use the shelter at No 13, Little Booba's.

For those Londoners who didn't have a back garden, of course, Anderson shelters were an impracticality, and few East Enders possessed a back garden; so the Government decided on the mass evacuation of the most vulnerable – children, pregnant women, mothers with babies and pre-school children, taking them out of densely populated areas like the East End and the docks and into the presumed safety of the countryside: moving no fewer than three-quarters of a million people in a mass military-style exercise. Markmanor Avenue and Clapton were not in the East End and the Teslers and the Chasons were not among those scheduled for evacuation, but we still felt vulnerable enough to want to get out of London. And so did young Winnie. While she went back to the safety of her home in Wales, we decided on a little evacuation of our own. On his salesman travels, Uncle Mick had found a little house to rent on the Micklefield Estate, a new building development on the outskirts of High Wycombe; and on Friday, September 1, 1939, the two families piled into his white van and made their way into the countryside.

In actual fact, Micklefield Estate itself – a vast area of new, characterless houses in a grid of rigidly straight streets – was considerably less rural than Markmanor Avenue; but our house was at the end of the estate and beyond us were the woods and fields of Buckinghamshire.

By the Sunday morning of that first weekend, the families having sorted out the accommodation and finished the unpacking, Stella and Eve prepared lunch while Rosalind and I and little Derek went exploring. We wandered for hours, collecting baskets of delicious cob nuts, this being the season for them, and made our way back to our new home in the glorious autumn sunshine. We were greeted with gloomy faces. This was Sunday, the third of September, 1939; Prime Minister Chamberlain had made a statement on the radio that morning: England was now at war with Germany.

And…?

And nothing happened.

No air-raids. No bombs. No poison gas.

Theatres and cinemas were closed by Government order to avoid exposing large crowds to aerial attacks; street and shop lights had to be extinguished at night; greyhound racing and other floodlit evening sports were suspended; a strict domestic blackout was imposed – house windows were masked with thick curtains, cardboard screens, blinds, even black paint – so that German bombers couldn't be guided by the glow to their targets at night. Food prices began to rise and food shortages occur because merchant ship cargos had to concentrate on goods for war rather than for consumption.

And nothing happened.

Early in the New Year, butter, bacon and sugar were rationed, and my mother made a patriotic gesture as her initial contribution to the war effort: for the duration of the conflict, bacon would be allowed in the house. Taxes were increased on sugar, beer and tobacco, partly because of the shortages, partly to help pay for the war. And still nothing happened. We had sent an army over to France – the British Expeditionary Force – but it wasn't engaged in any fighting: the British and French armies were on watch behind the impregnable Maginot Line of fortresses protecting France from Germany. But there were no air engagements, no sea battles, no Nazi onslaught. The newspapers began to call this The Phoney War: why on earth did we have to suffer all these deprivations? What were we making these sacrifices *for*?

Within weeks the theatres and cinemas were open again. By Christmas half the evacuees had drifted back to London, including the Chasons. The Teslers stayed on for a few weeks longer. It was impractical to maintain a house just for the four of us, so we knocked on doors and found a family on the edge of the estate that would rent us a room in their little bungalow. Our accommodation was cramped; the bungalow was in the middle of a plot of totally uncultivated land – no, not land: *earth*; the family kept chickens – scores and scores of chickens; the weather was atrocious, and the earth surrounding the bungalow quickly turned to mud. All I remember of that awful period is mud, rain and the all-pervading smell and sight of chicken-pooh. I couldn't wait to get home, which we did before the end of the year.

But then, suddenly, in April 1940 the phoney war became very real. The Germans invaded Denmark and Norway. A British force despatched to Norway was summarily repelled; the disaster forced the resignation of Chamberlain as Prime Minister and the appointment of Winston Churchill – the one bright spark in the encircling gloom. The impregnability of the Maginot Line was never tested: at the beginning of May, Germany simply ignored it, invaded Belgium and Holland and turned south behind the Line through Belgium to invade France. The Allies had been outflanked and out-manoeuvred, and were suddenly on the run.

Our newspaper headlines grew blacker each day. The jaunty tones of the newsreel commentators in the cinemas became more and more grave. Fighting the fiercest of rearguard battles, the Allied forces retreated towards the French coast; and at the end of May we began to evacuate them from Dunkirk and other ports along the coast. Under ferocious attack by land, sea and air, half a million Allied servicemen were rescued from the beaches by a hastily recruited armada of warships, tugs, trawlers, fishing boats, any seagoing vessel that could make it across the Channel.

The evacuation was a miraculous achievement, and it brought the gloomy, grumbling nation together in an extraordinary way. This is what the sacrifices and deprivations had been for. Poland, Belgium, Denmark, Norway, Holland and now France had surrendered; Mussolini's Italy had joined Germany and declared war on us: suddenly, Britain stood alone; and a remarkable spirit of resistance seized the nation.

Churchill promised us blood, sweat and tears in a struggle against enormous odds, but somehow we felt we could overcome those odds no matter how long it took us. This was 'the Dunkirk spirit', a phrase coined by J.B. Priestley in his BBC broadcasts after the Nine O'clock News, to which we in Markmanor Avenue listened intensely; and it was reflected in the new tone of defiance in the newspapers, the renewed strength and confidence in the voices of the newsreel commentators. You felt it in the cinemas as the audiences cheered the shots of Churchill and the Royal family; I felt it in the talk among my friends at school; my father and I felt it in the atmosphere of those conversations at the garden gate with neighbours in our evening walks. And we certainly needed that spirit: we all knew it was only a matter of time before the Nazis would attempt to invade us.

But first they had to achieve mastery of the air over Britain, which they had failed to do in the skies over Dunkirk; and for a month, between the middle of August and the middle of September 1940, the Battle of Britain raged over south-eastern England as the Luftwaffe tried to destroy R.A.F. Fighter Command by bombing its airfields and radar installations. For the nation, and especially the small boys like me and my friends, this was a nail-biting but exhilarating time as the Spitfires and Hurricanes of the Royal Air Force took on the previously all-conquering might of the German Luftwaffe, monitored by the daily newspapers, by radio broadcasts and most vividly by the cinema newsreels, where we cheered at the sight and sound of aerial dogfights, of Messerschmitts and Heinkels exploding in the air or spiralling down to crash in the sea or on the ground.

Hundreds of planes were destroyed – 1,793 German, 915 British – and many brave airmen on both sides lost their lives. We didn't know until well after the end of the war just how close-run the Battle of Britain had actually been. It ended because Hitler decided that Goering's Luftwaffe couldn't achieve the air superiority over south-east England necessary for a successful invasion to take place and also, incredibly enough, because of an operational error on the part of a few Heinkel bomber pilots.

In a raid at the end of August, chased and harried by British fighters, some of the Heinkels lost their way and dumped their bombs on London instead of an RAF airfield. A few nights later, to bolster British morale, Bomber Command attacked Berlin in retaliation. Incensed at the sheer audacity of the British – how dare they! the Royal Air Force should have been on its knees by now! – Hitler ordered the Luftwaffe to switch its attacks to London. Just in time: the RAF wasn't quite on its knees, but by the beginning of September Fighter Command's reserves of pilots and aircraft were dangerously low.

On the afternoon of Saturday September 7 1940, my father and I were sitting in one of Leyton's plusher cinemas watching Night Train To Munich, a first-rate espionage thriller directed by Carol Reed. It was – and still is – a most enjoyable film and we were in a great mood as we left the cinema, a mood enhanced by the glorious sunset that confronted us on the horizon as we emerged. And then we realised that we were facing south not west and it was too early for sunset anyway. These were not the sun's rays staining the skies a deep flickering red, and that wasn't the horizon: this was London, *burning*.

No wonder the extraneous traffic noise had seemed particularly loud during the film. It wasn't traffic noise. While we were watching Night Train To Munich, 400 German bombers and more than 600 fighters had set London's docks and the East End in which they were situated ablaze, and the fires were still burning when another wave of 200 bombers attacked again that night. This was Black Saturday. The Blitz had begun.

The Blitz

It continued for nine horrendous months. London's fears and imaginings, like that opening sequence of Things To Come, were only too painfully realised: the bombers did get through. Relentlessly, night after night for the first sixty-seven nights and in daytime too, they got through; and they rained their high explosive and incendiary bombs down on an almost defenceless capital.

The fighters of our depleted Air Force were blind at night; the hundreds of great, elephantine barrage balloons above the city were effective only against low-flying aircraft, and these bombers didn't fly low; our anti-aircraft batteries were ineffectively deployed and their sound-location equipment less than adequate. There weren't enough air-raid shelters and, because it had been presumed that the attacks would come in daylight, those shelters that did exist had no provision for eating or sleeping and little or no toilet facilities. Our emergency services were inexperienced – how could they have been otherwise? – and they were unprepared for the devastation that the raids would cause. London's fire brigades were stretched to breaking-point. Nurses in the East End's first-aid posts were overwhelmed by the walking wounded. Ambulances couldn't get through the blazing, broken streets. Rescue squads working through the night were swamped by the immensity of their task as they tried to free families trapped in the debris of their shattered homes.

Having failed to destroy RAF Fighter Command, Hitler's plan was to undermine the nation's will to resist invasion by razing our cities to the ground, starting with the capital itself. He got perilously near to succeeding. We didn't know it at the time but the Battle of London was as close-run a thing as the Battle of Britain. Thousands of Londoners were killed; hundreds of thousands of houses destroyed; by the middle of October 250,000 people had been made homeless.

Without a roof over their heads, and with hopelessly inadequate facilities for shelter – in some areas like West Ham there were hardly any air-raid shelters at all – thousands of East End families fled to the countryside, like the convoys of refugees we'd seen in the newsreels only months before, thronging the roads of

France as the German armies advanced.

They camped out in Epping Forest and in the hopfields of Kent. They broke into the cavern complex at Chislehurst: after one week of the Blitz 8,000 Londoners were living in these caves; by the end of October there were 15,000. In mid-September, thousands of East Enders stormed their local tube stations to use them as shelters: within days, more than 150,000 were sheltering in the Underground, the authorities powerless to move them. Disillusioned and discontented, surrounded by chaos and confusion, there were times, particularly in the early weeks of that relentless nightly devastation, when London's morale was in very real danger of cracking.

That it didn't crack was, like Dunkirk, the stuff of miracles. As destruction spread from the East End and the docks to the City, the West End and the more prosperous areas of Belgravia and Kensington – even Buckingham Palace and the Houses of Parliament were hit – the sense of shared suffering began to generate a feeling of communal solidarity.

Augmented by many thousands of volunteers, the emergency services began to cope with their enormous task. The London Fire Brigade, with 2000 professional fire-fighters and no fewer than 23,000 auxiliaries, became folk heroes, along with the capital's hard-pressed doctors and nurses. The ranks of the rescue squads and repair gangs were joined by thousands of voluntary supporters. Women were driving fire engines and ambulances, staffing the emergency control centres and acting as despatch riders. Thousands of air-raid wardens, 90% of them voluntary part-timers, co-ordinated an increasingly well-organised air-defence system. The Government got its act together and took over from inefficient local councils the task of housing the homeless, setting up mobile washing vans to do their laundry for free and establishing public canteens where the food was nutritious and cheap. The Army was called in to help repair damaged homes. Adequate sleeping facilities, toilets and hot meals began to be provided in the air-raid shelters both above and below ground. People took the initiative and began to form themselves into street committees for firewatching duties and shelter committees to organise sleeping and toilet arrangements in the Underground.

Londoners began to adapt. The courage of the emergency services and the order that began to emerge out of the chaos helped to create a growing stoicism among Londoners. The RAF night fighters were withdrawn and our anti-aircraft batteries, now more effectively deployed and with improved equipment, were free to blaze away at the bombers with a stupendous nightly barrage that might not have downed many Heinkels but gave a great boost to Londoners' morale.

People ignored the air-raid sirens during the day and carried on going to work as normal – there were no labour stoppages or strikes during the blitz. It was business as usual in the shops: with their plate glass windows blown to smithereens, shopkeepers would put up signs like 'More Open Than Usual' and 'Blast!' Normal life continued, underground if necessary: by the spring of 1941 the caves at Chislehurst had been transformed into a subterranean city, offering its shelterers a range of services including canteens, a hospital and a cinema. Borough councils set up evening classes, discussion groups and concerts in shelters both under and above ground. The proud boast was London Can Take It! and newsreel and press coverage ensured that the entire world was aware of that fact as well as Londoners themselves.

On October 12 Hitler called off Operation Sea Lion, his planned invasion of Britain. On November 14, for the first time since early September, the Luftwaffe didn't bomb London: it turned its attention to Coventry and devastated that city overnight. From now on, London was to share the burden of air attacks with the rest of the major industrial centres of Britain, although it still had to endure more raids and bombs than any other. Throughout the spring of 1941 the capital continued to suffer death and destruction almost nightly and the attacks became progressively heavier, culminating in an onslaught on May 10 that was the most ferocious of the entire blitz.

On that night, London was set ablaze from Hammersmith in the west to Romford in the east; more civilians were killed – 1,436 – than in any other single raid on Britain; the damage to houses and buildings and the city's gas and electricity infrastructure was colossal. If a raid of such vicious brutality had hit the capital nine months earlier it might well have delivered the knock-out blow Hitler was seeking when he began the Battle of London. But Londoners had learned to live with the blitz by now: London really could take it. The bombers didn't return the next night; or the next. Having failed to bomb London into submission, Hitler was about to present them with another task. On 22 June Germany invaded Russia, and the Luftwaffe flew east.

The Teslers At War

What was happening to the Teslers during this harrowing period?

Incredibly, Walthamstow was unscathed during the early weeks of the blitz. As far as we knew, not a bomb fell on it. Every evening, when the air-raid sirens wailed – terrifying sound! – we made our way to Little Booba's at No 13 and into her Anderson shelter – six feet high, six feet long, four feet six inches wide

– which the council workmen had sunk into her little garden.

The five of us – Mum, Dad, Rosalind, Little Booba and me – would squeeze into the chairs at the end of the shelter and the wooden benches on either side, made up with sheets and blankets and pillows, and try to sleep while the bombers droned above us, the crump of their bombs reverberating in the distance and the anti-aircraft guns creating a non-stop, eardrum-cracking racket over our heads. We had a chamber pot down there for emergencies, but we tried not to use it; instead, we used to make a breathless dash for the lavatory inside No 13, our torches lighting the way if the moon wasn't shining, the anti-aircraft searchlights sweeping the sky, catching barrage balloons and sometimes a Nazi bomber in their beams, the anti-aircraft shells bursting overhead, the dreadful noise of their guns deafening us as we bolted for the house.

And in the morning, as the sirens sounded the blissful All Clear, we'd gather ourselves together, say goodbye to Little Booba and make our way home again to wash and brush up and have a little breakfast; and then for me it was off to school, for my father off to his millinery factory in the City. And as he travelled to work by bus and tram through the bomb-cratered streets my father would see the evidence each day of the death and destruction inflicted on London every night.

For me and my friends, however, this was another thrilling and exhilarating time. At night we read our comics by torchlight in our Anderson Shelters, listening to our anti-aircraft batteries blasting the German bombers out of the sky as we patriotically believed, defying the Luftwaffe every time we ran to the loo inside our houses. During the day, when we weren't at school, we'd hunt for bits of shrapnel from ack-ack shells in the fields around Markmanor Avenue or peer through the gaps in the fences surrounding the barrage-balloon bases in our area; or sometimes, if we were lucky, when there were daylight raids and we could watch the vapour trails of aerial dogfights in the sky above us, we would cheer our Spitfires and Hurricanes because we knew from the radio and newspapers and newsreels that they were winning the war in the air. And so they were, though not at all by the margin we believed at the time.

And then, one night early in the November of 1940, the noise of aircraft and guns and exploding bombs seemed louder and nearer to No.13 than usual; and when the All Clear sounded and we walked back up the Avenue to our own house we could see neighbours gathered in the street and a rescue team at work in front of some heavily damaged houses a few doors further up. Markmanor Avenue had suffered a direct hit; and though no-one had been hurt and No.44 had suffered no damage whatsoever, the Blitz didn't seem quite so exciting anymore. My parents thought it was time for another evacuation, and quick. Within days, friends of my parents, Mr and Mrs Lewin, had closed up their flat in the Finchley Road and collected us in their large saloon car and we were on our way to High Wycombe once more. I could not know, and would not have believed, that we would never return to live in No. 44, or Markmanor Avenue, or Walthamstow again.

Back To Bucks

The Lewins had heard from friends that Holmer Green, a little village between High Wycombe and Amersham in Buckinghamshire, was a pleasant place in which to live, and since this time we had no Uncle Mick to pre-plan and pre-arrange our accommodation, the four adults decided that we would simply drive there and knock on doors, as we ourselves had done the previous year at the end of our stay on the Micklefield Estate.

Mr and Mrs Lewin fairly quickly found a cottage in Holmer Green itself that could take in the two of them, but it wasn't so easy for a family of four: this was a small village with small dwelling-places and we exhausted its possibilities in only an hour or so of fruitless knocking on doors; so we decided to look beyond it. The Lewins drove us around until we discovered a pleasant little lane just outside the village off the road to High Wycombe, with a white-washed house at the end of it which seemed large enough to accommodate another four people. We knocked on the door and, weary and despondent by now, explained our problem.

The very pleasant lady of the house, Mrs Salethorn, invited us in for a cup of tea and having given us the once-over said she thought that, since her husband was away in the Army, her daughter Jean could sleep in her bedroom, so if the four of us were prepared to share the other bedroom we might all be able to make a go of it. The Teslers could more or less take over the sitting room although Jean, who was about a year older than me, would have to come into it to practise her piano-playing; and we could share the scullery and the kitchen, which was furnished with a large table and enough chairs for us all to have our meals around it.

"And the bathroom?" my mother asked.

"Bless you, there's no bathroom: you won't find a bathroom anywhere in the village, my dears; we bring the tin bath into the scullery from the garden shed whenever we need a bath and fill it with water we've boiled up on the kitchen range – but there's a basin in the bedroom and a jug that you can fill from the scullery tap so you can wash yourselves any time you like."

"A jug and basin?"

"Yes dear."

"And" – my mother said, rather quaveringly – "the toilet?"

"Oh that's outside of course."

"Yes. Of course."

And so it was; a little wooden hut, with a little wooden seat, and torn-up newspapers on a hook for lavatory paper, and no chain to pull because there was no running water: the bucket had to be emptied regularly into a covered cess-pit in a neighbouring field which council workers cleared every week or so. Ah well, we felt, if that's how you live in the country, that's how the Teslers will have to live. And that's how we did live for the next two years.

Once we had sorted ourselves out and fallen into a practical routine, they were good and happy years. The bed in our bedroom was just about big enough to accommodate my parents, and my father in any case was going to have to spend his weekdays in London, coming out by train and bus to join us at the weekend. They bought camp-beds for Rosalind and me; and any family belongings that wouldn't fit into the chest of drawers and wardrobe in our bedroom were installed in the sitting room below.

We got on well with the Salethorns and happily ate our meals together during the week, joined by Corporal Salethorn on the rare occasions that he was on leave; at the weekends, when my father was with us, the Salethorns would let the Teslers catch up on their respective weekday news and had their meals separately at different times. The village was a pretty and friendly one, well served by buses that ran between High Wycombe and Amersham. High Wycombe itself was an agreeable market town with good shops and three cinemas; the countryside surrounding us was beautiful and welcoming; the air was fresh and clean. And it was so quiet: there were no air-raids, no anti-aircraft guns to disturb our sleep…

But shouldn't I be going to school?

School Days

"Right! Get Your Cap!"

I had very much enjoyed my years at Sybourn Street Elementary School, though I remember little of its details. I know I was successful academically, usually coming somewhere at the top of my class in several of the subjects; and I did well enough in what was the equivalent of today's Eleven Plus for my head teacher to recommend that I sit the entrance exam for the local grammar school, the Sir George Monoux in Walthamstow, which I did and passed.

And I got on swimmingly with the boys and girls in my Sybourn Street class. There's a jolly little picture of us at the age of eight or nine, so many of the faces familiar to me though I can't remember all their names – but isn't that Jackie Shafron on my right hand; and Harold Eckert at the left of the front row and Tony Manzi at the right; and Louis Edmonds top left? And isn't that darkly handsome boy three faces in on the next row little Philip Solomons, in whose house I used to play and whose father, a more recent immigrant from Russia than mine, always used to say in his thick Russian accent when it was time for me to go home and Philip's toys were still sprawled all over their sitting-room floor, "Phillie, put avay der rubbish!"?

All those sweet little faces, all those characters and personalities already formed, most of whom you suspect will look exactly the same today, only older. I remember just one fight in my six years at Sybourn Street. It was with an older boy from another class. He was the red-headed son of Harry Pollitt, the leader of the British Communist Party, and I considered it my patriotic duty to confront him on 23 August 1939, the day we heard that Communist Russia had signed a non-aggression pact with Britain's arch-enemy Hitler. The fight was a draw; where was Jack Greenstock when I needed him?

Sir George Monoux Grammar was a very different proposition, however. It was clearly more upmarket than Sybourn Street and it wasn't at all welcoming. It was an all-boys school, and I was used to learning and mixing with girls as well as boys. I was also used to a school where children of different religions – Jewish, Protestant, Catholic – happily and unquestioningly mingled. I was now in a school where I appeared to be the only Jewish boy. In the school playground, during the mid-morning break a few days into the beginning of that autumn term of 1939, I found myself in the middle of a ring of threatening, grim-faced eleven-year olds who were calling me "Jew boy!" and accusing me of having killed Jesus Christ: I mean, literally, they were crying out "You killed Jesus! You killed Jesus!" Me? Me, personally? I didn't know what on earth they were talking about.

It was my first experience of anti-Semitism. I have only ever had one other, and I could understand the reason for that. It was seven years later, when I was a National Serviceman in the army in Rhyl. Jewish underground militants in Palestine were fighting for independence from British military rule, and in retaliation for the execution by hanging of three of their comrades had captured and killed two British army sergeants, hanging them in a public market-place. There was inevitably bitter resentment among my fellow soldiers, manifested, since I was the only Jew conveniently to hand, in baleful glances and mutterings of "Dirty Jew!" directed at me for a while, until they realised I was a decent enough mate and could hardly be blamed personally for what was going on in the Middle East. I could understand their behaviour and very much sympathise with it; I simply couldn't understand the behaviour of my well-educated fellow pupils in a smart, civilised grammar school in 20th century London.

I went home for lunch that day very unhappy indeed, and it didn't take my mother long to realise that something was wrong. It took her even less time to persuade me to tell her what had happened; whereupon she said "Right! Get your cap!", put on her coat, marched me back to school, demanded to see the head and gave him a large and forceful piece of her mind. He apologised for the behaviour of what he was certain was only a small and untypical group of pupils and said he would see that it didn't happen again. I had to tell him the names of those responsible and he obviously had a word with them, and it didn't happen again; but now I had the reputation of being a sneak, and a baby for having to have my mother fight my battles for me, and the school became even less congenial than before.

What was it John Betjeman said in his mock denunciation of wartime Slough – "Come, friendly bombs, and fall on Slough"? The bomb that dropped on Markmanor Avenue was friendly for me as well as timely: it rescued me from a school in which I never felt comfortable and which was never likely to help me realise whatever potential I might have possessed. But was I going to be any more fortunate with a Buckinghamshire alternative?

There were secondary grammar schools in both Amersham and High Wycombe, but High Wycombe was nearer and the Royal Grammar School in High Wycombe sounded grander, so when my mother thought I'd had more than enough time away from study it was to the Royal Grammar School that we took ourselves for an interview with its Head.

The interview was pleasant enough, but at the end of it the Head informed us that, alas, his school was completely full and there was no room for me in it. However, the reason why the Royal Grammar School was short of space was because a London Grammar School had been evacuated to it and was currently occupying a third of its classrooms; and this school, the Chiswick County School for Boys, might possibly have a place for me. So, a phone call from one Head to another, a walk along the corridor to another part of the building, an interview with another Headmaster, the formidable Dr Carran, and I was in. The former pupil of a snooty, anti-Semitic East London school was now a pupil of a totally unfamiliar West London school billeted on another school in the middle of the Buckinghamshire countryside. Had I gone from the frying-pan to the fire?

In one glorious, liberating, energising word: No. In the months that followed, I found to my delight that Chiswick County was a marvellous school: friendly, receptive, with enlightened teachers, a decent but not exacting standard of sport and physical training and a reputation for first-class school plays, which instinctively intrigued me. On that first interview day, Dr Carran showed my mother and me round the school, and in the assembly hall we saw the boys rehearsing a production of Julius Caesar with impressive scenery and full stage lighting. Now *this* was a school! As for anti-Semitism: I discovered in due course that nearly half the boys in the class I was to join were Jewish; I never experienced anti-Semitism in school again.

Country Life

The next two years were pretty idyllic. I enjoyed school, and got on well with both teachers and fellow-pupils. Once we had accustomed ourselves to the rural way of life in Holmer Green the family found it pleasant and relaxing. Rosalind was happy in the village school; we got used to having our weekly baths in the tin tub dragged into the kitchen; we even got used to the outside loo, though we cursed it in the winter months. There was always a good movie on in one or other of High Wycombe's three cinemas. The BBC had launched a morale-boosting new radio service – The Forces Programme – introducing us for the first time to legendary American radio series like The Bob Hope Show, The Jack Benny Show and The Fred Allen Show as well as its own new wartime light entertainment productions like Garrison Theatre, Happidrome, ITMA and Much

Binding In The Marsh.

My interest in aeroplanes, inspired by the newsreel pictures of Spitfires and Hurricanes versus Heinkels, Dorniers and Messerschmitts in the Battle of Britain, was stimulated by the great variety of British and, later, American aircraft in the busy skies above Buckinghamshire. I bought the magazines Flight and The Aeroplane every week and started up an aircraft-spotting team with some of my school friends: we were good enough to challenge the local Royal Observer Corps team and win.

My father spent every weekend with us, and every now and again he would take us all to the movies in High Wycombe, sometimes including the Salethorns. I remember the joint excursion – including Jean's father who was on leave that weekend – to the Rex to see Charlie Chaplin's The Great Dictator early in 1941. Dad was particularly pleased with that film, not just because he thought Chaplin was funny and its satirical treatment of Hitler and Mussolini inspiring but because he was proud that this genius Chaplin was Jewish. Jewish people like to think that their heroes, especially the artistic ones, are also Jewish, and that's particularly easy to believe of film stars, so: "Did you know that Tony Curtis is Jewish? And Lauren Bacall? And Leslie Howard? and Kirk Douglas? and Hedy Lamarr?" In actual fact, all these others were or are Jewish; Chaplin wasn't.

The raids on London had eased though by no means ceased after the German invasion of Russia in June 1941; but even if we had wanted to there was no question of our returning to Walthamstow. The severe housing shortage created by the Blitz had prompted tough new Government regulations, making it mandatory for unoccupied houses to be taken over by families in need of accommodation, and No. 44 Markmanor Avenue was no longer occupied, even by my father on weekdays. In the early days of the air-raids he had moved his parents out of the East End into a large old house overlooking Clapton Common in Stamford Hill, which was where he stayed during the week; and now he was obliged to let our old home to a bombed-out family at a nominal rent.

Booba and Zaida were comfortable in their house in Stamford Hill and had had no desire to return to village life when we embarked on our second evacuation, any more than Little Booba had been prepared to leave her house and belongings in Markmanor Avenue. So the house on Clapton Common was our base whenever we came up to London, which we often did, especially during school holidays. I was perfectly happy about that: the Hackney Empire and Holborn Empire were more accessible than they had been to Walthamstow; there were two excellent local cinemas in Stamford Hill, and I had been introduced to the first-run cinemas in the West End: my mother took Rosalind and me to see

Disney's Pinocchio and Dumbo at the New Gallery Cinema in Oxford Street and by the end of 1941 I was making the journey from Stamford Hill to the West End by myself.

I discovered that at some of the West End's first-run cinemas – particularly the Plaza in the Haymarket but also the Empire and its next-door neighbour in Leicester Square, the Ritz – the Friday morning performances were frequently preceded by trade previews of even newer forthcoming films, so my Friday was often made up of a double-header at the Plaza in the morning, followed by a sandwich and a cup of coffee in an ABC or Lyons tea-room, followed by an afternoon session at the Empire or the Odeon in Leicester Square before embarking on the bus or tube journey back to Stamford Hill. If necessary, I could always fill in an hour between movie-houses by popping into a newsreel cinema, which provided a day-long continuous performance of an hour or so of cartoons, newsreels, special subjects and two-reeler comedies – some of them, my favourites, showing nothing but cartoons alongside the news.

There were a dozen or so of these little cinemas in Piccadilly and Leicester Square and near the tube stations in central London, used by travellers to kill time between trains, shoppers to rest their feet, office-workers to divert them over their lunchtime sandwich. And small boys who just liked watching anything that moved on the screen.

"Today I Am A Man"

Those trips to London were not exclusively devoted to the cinema, however. My Barmitzvah was due in the February of 1942 on my 13th birthday, when in the Jewish tradition I would formally become an adult; and I prepared for it by taking lessons with a rabbi who came to my grandparents' house during the summer, autumn and Christmas breaks from school in 1941, and with another rabbi in High Wycombe, who kept me up to speed in the little synagogue there between our London visits.

Oddly enough, the ceremony itself was announced as a Confirmation not a Barmitzvah on the invitations – I thought that Confirmation was the name for coming of age in the Progressive rather than the Orthodox tradition and that it took place on one's 15th not 13th birthday but of course, true to form, it never occurred to me to ask my parents why it was being announced that way. At any rate, it took place on 28 February 1942, the nearest available Saturday to my birthday on the 19th, in the venerable old Orthodox synagogue in Vine Court, Whitechapel. I have very little recollection of it, except that the synagogue was crowded and noisy and bright and I seemed to sing my portion of the Torah acceptably: at any rate, when I'd finished there were lots of cries of "*Sh'coyech!*", the Hebrew equivalent of "Good on you!" and "More strength to your elbow!".

I recollect even less of the celebratory dinner that followed the ceremony, although I know from the menu preserved among my papers that it was probably as slap-up a do as you could provide in those austere times. It took place the following day, Sunday March 1st, at lunchtime at Stern's Hotel in Mansell Street, just around the corner from the Synagogue – next day at lunchtime rather than after the Sabbath on the barmitzvah day itself because of the risk of night-time air-raids. But it was still billed on the Menu as a Dinner, given by Mr and Mrs D. Tesler on the occasion of the Confirmation of their son, at 2pm sharp, Reception at 12.30 pm; and it ran to seven courses if you follow the lay-out on the Menu: Cocktail; Hors d'Oeuvres Variés; Vermicelli Soup and Almonds; Roast Chicken, Croquette Potatoes, Green Peas; Salad; Wonder Ice Gateaux; Plums; and Black Coffee. I think the Ice Gateaux was called "Wonder" because meat – chicken – was on the menu and, this being a kosher affair and Stern's being kosher caterers, there could be no dairy products in the same meal, so the ice cream gateaux had to be made without ice cream. Seems pretty wonderful to me.

And now I was a man. Officially. I didn't feel very different; except that I began to notice girls; or at least *a* girl: Jean, our landlady's daughter. To be correct, Jean began to notice me: suddenly, on Saturday afternoons, when I walked down the lane to catch the bus to go to the pictures in High Wycombe, Jean was walking down the lane behind me and catching the bus too; and – what a coincidence! – the film I was going to see was the one that she had wanted to see too, so why not see it together? So, gradually, we started to go to the pictures together and go for walks together and bicycle rides into the country together and yes, we became sweet on each other as the saying goes. My mother wasn't very happy about it: "Watch out, you, or you'll find yourself on the front page of The News Of The World, God forbid!" But my little liaison with Jean completed the idyll of that spring and summer of 1942.

It wasn't to last.

The Chiswick County School for Boys had evacuated itself to the safety of the countryside – first to Amersham, then to High Wycombe – at the beginning of the war, as so many schools had done. Not all its pupils had chosen to go with it and by the Christmas of 1939, when the war still appeared phoney, some of those who fled to the country had drifted back to London with their families, which is why there had been room in its High Wycombe complement for me.

Those who had stayed in Chiswick and those who had gone back to join them needed to continue their education, but they couldn't use the School's premises in Burlington Lane because the Office of Works had requisitioned them for the Government. An alternative home had been found in the old Victorian building vacated by Isleworth County School when its own new School was completed, and a nucleus of staff was seconded from High Wycombe to organise and run this rump of Chiswick County there. But now, early in 1942, the Chiswick School's own buildings were being relinquished by the Government, so at the end of the Spring term it was able to announce that at the beginning of the Autumn term both its sections would be going back to Chiswick to be united once again on their old site.

My parents found themselves in a serious dilemma. I was very happy at Chiswick County and working well in it. What were they to do? Remain in Holmer Green and get me into the Royal Grammar School, to start all over again with new teachers and new schoolmates? Go back to Walthamstow to pick up where I had left off in a school with unhappy memories of both teachers and pupils? What they did, and what I will always be profoundly grateful for, was remarkable.

They decided that the family would go back to Chiswick with the County School.

Dave and Stella would tear up their East End roots and move to the other side of London – the other side of the moon as far as they were concerned – to a West London suburb of which they knew nothing and where they knew nobody, simply to ensure that their son could continue his education with a school he was happy in. Dave would have to travel across London to and from his millinery business every working day for the rest of his life, and he and Stella would have to start their social lives all over again in what must have seemed like a foreign country. But their son would owe everything in his future education and professional career to that sacrifice. And he would never forget it.

Beginning Again

During that summer my parents found a flat in Watchfield Court, an attractive modern block built in the late thirties at the top end of Sutton Court Road. They couldn't have chosen a better location. Chiswick was then – and very much remains – a pleasant, leafy West London suburb, with a busy High Street full of good and varied shops and an excellent Public Library. It also had three cinemas within easy reach and – a big plus for the Tesler family – a music hall theatre, the

Chiswick Empire, a distinguished member of the Moss Empire circuit to which the much loved Hackney and Holburn Empires also belonged. The Empire was just across the green from our block of flats; Chiswick Park and Turnham Green Underground stations were within easy walking distance and Chiswick Swimming Baths were only a short bus-ride away.

Within the radius of a 15-minute trolley-bus ride were Kew, with its fabulous Gardens and the little Q Theatre; Richmond, with its ice-rink, the river and the Richmond Theatre; Hammersmith, with two cinemas and two more theatres, the King's and the Lyric; and Shepherds Bush, with another cinema and another Moss Circuit music hall, the Shepherds Bush Empire. The glittering delights of the West End were a mere half-hour away by Tube. Most important, Chiswick County School for Boys was only a ten minute walk from Watchfield Court, on the other side of Chiswick House and its grounds, through which I would go to and from school for the next four years.

We were introduced to Chiswick House, Lord Burlington's stunning 18th century Palladian villa, on the afternoon of our first day in Watchfield Court, in the late summer of 1942. Another Jewish couple in the block, Mr and Mrs Citron, had spotted us: Jewish antennae are finely tuned; they welcomed the family to the flats and asked if we'd like to join them for tea in the cricket pavilion in the House grounds. Their two sons, ex-pupils of Chiswick County, were playing for the old boys, the Old Meadonians, in a match against the school and it would give us a chance to look at Chiswick House itself and explore its lawns and gardens. It was a lovely, sunny September afternoon and we all strolled down Sutton Court Road, across Ellesmere Road, turned into Chesterfield Road, and crossed over to the Park Road entrance of Chiswick House. I couldn't possibly have imagined that sixty-four years later I'd still be walking through that Park Road entrance almost every day. The pavilion was packed, the company was welcoming, the House and its grounds were enchanting. We could not have had a more auspicious beginning to our new life.

Number 89 Watchfield Court was a pleasant, light, south-facing apartment with two bedrooms, a sitting room, dining room, kitchen, bathroom and lavatory and an additional separate lavatory, all coming off the hall onto which the front door opened. The barmitzvah boy was awarded the second bedroom and Rosalind had to sleep in a separate bed in the main bedroom. Some time later, as she got older and our parents found her nightly presence increasingly inhibiting, the dining-room table was consigned to Dad's garage, Rosalind's bed was moved into the dining room and our meals were eaten in the kitchen.

Because the rooms were all a little smaller than their equivalents at 44 Markmanor Avenue and there was no box-room to provide a little extra space, quite a bit of room-juggling had to be done over the years. When I went into the Army at eighteen for my two years of National Service, Rosalind took over the second bedroom and the dining room got its table back again. Whenever I was home on leave, the table returned to the garage and – rather than periodically shift Rosalind about – I slept in the dining room.

I continued to sleep in the dining room: in the months between National Service and University, during the vacations of my three years at Oxford, for the four months between Oxford and the BBC, and for my first nine months at the BBC, until Rosalind got married in 1953. I was 24 years old before I got my bedroom back again, which I retained for the next seven years. That must seem pretty strange by today's standards, but in those days it wasn't at all unusual for sons as well as daughters to live at home until they were married – they still do so in Italian society and probably for the same reasons: free board, lodging and laundry. Well, in my case, not entirely free: once I had started to earn a salary at the BBC I paid my mother the munificent sum of £2 a week all in: a bargain if ever there was one, particularly because by that time my parents were going away on holiday a great deal so I often had the flat to myself for entertaining.

You can get used to anything – remember the tin bath and the outside loo in Holmer Green? – and sleeping in that dining-room wasn't too bad, except when my parents were doing their own entertaining in the sitting room and I was too tired not to go to bed. Only the folding doors dividing the two rooms separated me from their convivial card-evenings with the murmur of happy conversation, roars of laughter at my father's jokes and cries of "Solo!", "I go Mizaire!", "Abundance!" Just like those summer evenings in Markmanor Avenue when the murmur of neighbours and the rumble of lawnmowers used to keep me from my sleep – except now it wasn't school I had to get up for the next morning but the studio. Did Cecil B de Mille begin like this?

Naturally, as a first-floor flat No 89 possessed no garden – my father's green fingers had to apply themselves in due course to one of the allotments in lower Stavely Road – but it did have a narrow little balcony opening out from the French windows of the dining/bedroom, and I remember a window-box or two adorning it which my mother used to tend. The balcony could accommodate a couple of deckchairs but only sideways on, so if you wanted to sunbathe you had to switch from left deckchair to right deckchair to achieve anything like an even tan. I tried opening the French windows and positioning my deckchair in their centre so that I could face the sun, but because the balcony wasn't very deep half the deckchair had to extend into the dining room, at which point the wall above the French windows blocked out the sun from my chest upwards. Buster Keaton would have found an ingenious way of getting a tan in spite of these physical difficulties, but I was more Laurel and Hardy then, as I seem to have become again now, and I never managed to achieve it.

These disadvantages were minor, however, and No 89 became our family home, and a very happy one, for well over forty years. Rosalind was married from there; my father died and was buried from there; I lived at No 89 until just before I was married; and my mother lived there until she was 84, when it became too much for her to look after by herself and she moved into sheltered accommodation at Homecross House on the other side of Chiswick High Road.

Although my parents had not known a soul in Chiswick when we moved to Watchfield Court, before very long they had become well-loved members of a new and growing Jewish community, making many new friends while never losing any of their old ones. Two of those old friends, the Eckerts, my schoolfriend Harold's parents, actually left Walthamstow to join them in Watchfield Court, and Harold became a fellow pupil at the County School.

There were usually at least three card-tables of players making up the permanent floating Watchfield Court Solo School as it moved between apartments at least once a week, from the Teslers to the Eckerts, from the George Toppers to the Charles Toppers, from the Bergers to the Firemans and back to the Teslers again. Jack Eckert was a hairdresser; George and Charles Topper were hairdressers too, but in a very different league. They were Court Hairdressers by Royal Appointment, two elegant middle-aged brothers with gracious, good-natured wives, proprietors of an extremely upmarket hairdressing establishment in the West End: two dignified English gentlemen, always impeccably turned out – George with a fine grey military moustache – but they both still sounded like Phillie Solomons' father.

Forty years later I had dealings with a high-powered City entrepreneur who was running a bid for another ITV company franchise and asked me for a little advice. His name was Bruce Fireman, and he turned out to be the nephew of Solly and Dolly Fireman, honoured alumni of the Watchfield Court Solo School. He told me he used to dread going to visit his aunt and uncle because they took every opportunity to hold me up as an example to the growing lad: "Dave and Stella's boy, that's who you should be like, always working hard and doing well at school, not a no-goodnik like you."

Well, he turned out to be not such a badnik, but yes, I was doing well at school, although because I was enjoying it so much it didn't seem as if I was working particularly hard.

Chiswick County

The Boys School occupied half a large site on Burlington Lane, the other half being taken up by the County Girls School, which had also returned to its old home three years after evacuating to the country. They shared a single imposing, attractively designed building which had been constructed in 1925, separated by doors in the centre of each of the building's three floors and by an orchard in the middle of the spacious playing fields that surrounded it – playing fields which were now disfigured by the grass-covered domes of underground air-raid shelters which the local Council had considered it prudent to install. There were two entirely separate school entrances and no fraternisation of any kind was allowed, not even a wave, even if the girl you were waving at was your sister. In my case it wasn't my sister because Rosalind was going to Belmont Girls' School on the other side of Chiswick High Road.

Most of the reunited teaching staff I remember from 1942 and onwards had been with the School from its inauguration in 1925, like Charles Curran, the Headmaster who showed my mother and me round the School in High Wycombe, Alan Cooke the Deputy Head, who was to succeed him in 1944, and David Dutton the Science Master; others had joined the School in the thirties, like the History Master David Kitchen, the English Master Charles Garlick and, especially, the School Secretary Gwen Dickenson, who looked like a young Wendy Hiller and upon whom I rapidly developed an enduring crush: ah, how I remember those bewitching ankles, that pale blue angora sweater and my attempts to time my walk to School in the morning to match hers so that we could walk together through the enchanted greenery of Chiswick House – after all, she couldn't have been more than twice my age.

All those County School teachers were decent, capable, easygoing educationists of a pre-war kind that doesn't seem to exist any more: they treated us as intelligent human beings who meant well and tried hard, so we did. I was particularly inspired by Charles Garlick, who encouraged my interest in reading, channelled it into a love of English literature and in due course persuaded me that an Oxford degree in English was something to which I could quite reasonably aspire. And David Kitchen enhanced my interest in the theatre; he was the extremely able producer of the annual School Play and I was usually standing first in line for the auditions each year.

It paid off. In March of 1943, our very first year in Chiswick, I made my theatrical debut as the lead in Noah, Andre Obey's modern comedy about the Biblical character, his family and his relationship with God, anticipating by many years Tevye's dealings with the Deity in Fiddler On The Roof. "At the opening of the first scene" said the Brentford & Chiswick Times "one doubted whether the cheerful countenance of B.Tesler and his clear youthful voice would be able to carry this off. But he did. In his fights with the truculent Ham, or when indignant at the cynicism of his family, he became quite patriarchal. His display of emotion when describing how he saw the last of mankind, bar themselves, drowning, and again when his family set forth on their adventures with never a backward look at the old man to whom they owe so much, was remarkable." Aw, shucks...

Early 1943 also saw the first return of German bombers to London since the Blitz, in retaliation for our own bombing attacks on German cities. A particularly large basket of incendiaries exploded over the School one night, setting fire to the huts used by the playing-field groundsman and the School's Scout troop and damaging the School Hall and science laboratories: for days afterwards small boys hunted for bits of shrapnel, just as we had done in Walthamstow in 1940. But London's air defences had become very much more effective – they now included my father and his Solo School companions, who had become community firefighters, guarding Watchfield Court's roofs with their tin hats, stirrup pumps and buckets of water: we could all now feel a little safer in our beds.

Feeling The Pinch

We were feeling the pinch of war in other ways. After the Japanese attack on Pearl Harbour in December 1941 we had a new and powerful ally in the United States, and Montgomery had turned the tide against Rommel and the German Afrika Korps in North Africa at El Alamein; but the Japanese had overrun the Empire in the Far East and cut off our traditional supplies of rubber, tin, tea and sugar, and our Merchant Navy losses in the North Atlantic were escalating dangerously as German U-boats savaged the shipping lanes between America and ourselves.

The resultant shortages were making everyday life increasingly dour and austere. Soap was rationed. Paper was rationed, so newspapers now filled only four pages. Clothes rationing, introduced in 1942, was severely tightened: you could buy a cardigan or sweater only once every five years, an overcoat every seven years, a dress or a pair of trousers and jacket or a pair of underpants every two years. Food rationing had been extended from butter, bacon and sugar to many other foods, including meat, tinned goods, tea, jam, honey, marmalade, cheese, milk and – horror of horrors – sweets and chocolate (my granddaughters will be appalled to know that they would have been allowed the equivalent of only one small bar of chocolate a week each) – and there were long queues at the shops when word got round that a delivery of this or that or almost any item whatsoever had arrived.

You were allowed one egg per person per week – if you could find them – and even powdered eggs, the substitute for the real thing, were rationed to one packet every two months. We were encouraged to eat food that didn't have to be brought to us by sea, notoriously a bony fish given the exotic name of snoek (which actually belonged to a fish previously imported from South Africa but was now used to glamourise pike from our own lakes and rivers); and something called spam, tins of pale pink flabby processed meat – we didn't dare ask exactly *what* meat – and even that joined the list of rationed goods in due course. Bread, potatoes, fruit, offal and fish were off the ration, but apart from bread and potatoes, and a few basic vegetables like carrots and cabbage, they were very much a rarity – you seldom saw an orange, and bananas completely disappeared for the duration.

People had to do things for themselves. They made or renovated their own clothes, knitted their own sweaters, unravelled old pullovers to knit socks and scarves from the wool – and not just for themselves: they sent them to our forces overseas as well. Silk stockings were no longer available so young women painted stockings on their legs and drew lines down the backs of their calves to look like centre seams.

Encouraged by the Government to Dig for Victory, men and women grew their own vegetables in allotments that sprang up all over the capital to supplement their slender rations – hence my father's return to the soil in Stavely Road at weekends and in the long summer evenings. Some of them even reared their own dinners: back gardens in many suburbs were turned into mini-farmyards for chickens and pigs. Would my mother's patriotic acceptance of bacon have extended to keeping the pigs themselves, as a sort of living larder, if we'd still lived in Markmanor Avenue?

Petrol was rationed from the very beginning of the war and it had become increasingly difficult to find a service station with a supply: you could tell which garage had received a delivery by the long queue of cars waiting for their meagre quota. When we moved to Chiswick in 1942 my father acquired our first family car, a little black Morris Minor, HXF 693 (you never forget the registration number of your first car). In the same year, driving for non-essential journeys was banned, which put paid to visiting grandparents by car. My father's petrol ration was restricted to his journeys to and from business so our visits to Big and Little Booba and Zaida had to be by bus and tube – a pretty laborious process because these too were curtailed in order to preserve fuel and electricity. The grandparents must have visited us by the same means, though I imagine very rarely. Rosalind does remember one occasion on which she actually had to share her bedroom with Little Booba; heaven knows how we should have managed if Big Booba and Zaida had stayed overnight.

One Sunday morning in 1943 we had a phone call from Zaida to say that Big Booba wasn't feeling well and my father and I rushed to Stamford Hill not by bus or tube, which would have taken an eternity, but by our Morris Minor. Inevitably, since Sunday morning was an unlikely time for vital business journeys to be undertaken by little family cars with only a driver and small boy inside them, we were stopped by a policeman, who did not consider our journey essential; and in due course my father was summoned to appear before the Stipendiary Magistrate at Bow Street Magistrates Court, charged with the improper use of petrol.

This kindly gentleman was prepared to consider the mercy dash to my grandmother an extenuating circumstance and my father was let off with a token fine; but it was still a pretty traumatic experience to see him in the Bow Street dock. Perhaps I would have felt a little better if I had known that fifty years later I would be Chairman of the Lord Chancellor's Advisory Committee, responsible for recommending prospective Magistrates for appointment to all the Courts in Inner London – including Bow Street, which I would be visiting quite frequently to check on the progress of our recommendations. My father might have felt a little better too.

Back To The Boards

The School Play in February 1944 was a revival of their 1931 production of George Bernard Shaw's St Joan. "Perhaps the most satisfying performances of all" said the Brentford and Chiswick Times "come from C.A.Pocock as the Bishop of Beauvais and B.Tesler as the Inquisitor. Both of them really look the parts, and the long speeches of the latter in the trial scene are delivered with telling effect."

My father was tickled pink by my interest in drama. He liked a good play himself, as well as a good music hall bill; one of his favourite jokes was that having been brought up on the hyper-histrionics of the Yiddish theatre he preferred the old theatre-manager type of acting to all this modern naturalism because with players like Donald Wolfit and Robert Atkins you could *tell* they were acting.

He joined the Sunday Club at the Q, the little white-stuccoed theatre at the foot of Kew Bridge, and he and I used to go there after an early dinner for its Sunday evening performances.

We also regularly went up to the West End for a Saturday matinee, preceded by a roll-mop salad lunch in the Levy & Franks bar at the top of St Martin's Lane; and my first experience of opera was when my father took us all to the King's Theatre in Hammersmith to see the Carl Rosa Opera Company in their touring production of La Traviata – I remember so clearly the impact on my romantic little soul of the desperate ecstasy of the music in the last act as Alfredo rushes into dying Violetta's bedroom for "Parigi, o cara, noi lasceremo", still one of my favourite Verdi arias. The King's, like the Q, is long gone; Levy & Franks is still there and flourishing.

I wonder sometimes if my father got as much heartwarming pleasure from my enjoyment of those theatre visits as I did many years later when I had the opportunity to return the compliment. I particularly remember a family outing to Fiddler On The Roof at the Prince of Wales Theatre. My wife Audrey and I sat with my parents between us and I looked along the row to her at one moment and saw my father leaning forward, eyes shining like a child's, with a great big smile on his face, positively eating up the show, the music and Topol's performance. It wasn't the production that reduced me to tears that evening.

As well as St Joan, the Luftwaffe returned to Chiswick in the opening months of 1944. Hitler's fortunes on the continent had begun to falter. In Italy, the German army was coming under increasing pressure from the Allied forces advancing from their invasion bridgeheads in the South; on the Eastern Front, the Soviet Army was forcing the Germans back through the Ukraine; Hitler knew that an Allied invasion of France was inevitable and imminent and that it would be planned and prepared in London. He needed to disrupt those preparations, so he ordered every serviceable aircraft at Goering's disposal to attack the capital.

The raids brought death and destruction back to the city in what was to be called the 'baby blitz', and West London wasn't spared. On the evening of the Friday performance of St Joan Chiswick suffered several direct hits, but this didn't prevent large audiences turning up for the matinee and evening performances next day; the takings for this production easily established a record for the School. And London's greatly improved air defences took their toll of the bombers, as they had done in the attacks of early 1943. The damage inflicted on the capital was nothing like that of the blitz itself, and the raids petered out at the end of March. We didn't know it but very much worse was to come.

V For Vengeance

On June 6 1944 the Allies invaded France. Exactly one week later the first flying bomb hit London.

This was Hitler's V-1, the *Vergeltungswaffe*, his secret Vengeance Weapon: a pilotless plane with stubby little wings, launched from camouflaged bases in northern France. This precursor of today's Cruise missile, propelled by a flaming engine at its rear, was quite literally a flying bomb, a warhead of great explosive power designed to cut out over its pre-set target, hurtle to the ground and blow up on impact.

Flying bombs had a limited range and were used almost exclusively against the British capital, although the Luftwaffe adapted some Heinkel 111 bombers to carry them under their fuselage and launch them from the air – so our friend Wynne Rooms isn't imagining things when she remembers as a child seeing a flying bomb passing over her home in Sheffield on its way to some northern target or other. And perhaps the battered, disarmed flying bomb displayed in the courtyard of the pub outside Pickering, where Audrey and Simon and I used to stop for a meal on our way to Audrey's family home in Sleights, had actually come down in Yorkshire and not been brought all the way up from London as a trophy of war.

The V-1 and the other secret weapons to follow it were weapons of revenge for the Allied bombs that had rained down on German cities since 1942. Hitler presumably believed that although the Vengeance Weapons might not in themselves win the war, they might stave off defeat and enable Germany to win a negotiated peace from a position of strength. Meanwhile they could kill as many Londoners as possible and give a boost to German morale. Within three days, flying bombs were reaching the Greater London area at the rate of seventy-three a day; by the end of June it was a hundred a day, and their effect was devastating.

These bombs were more powerful than any that had fallen on London during the Blitz, and this time there was no air raid siren to warn us of an imminent attack: they were small and fast enough to avoid detection by radar. At any time of the day or night the only indication that death and destruction might be just seconds away was the sudden buzzing drone of an engine – was it approaching? was it receding? was it overhead? – then the heart-stopping engine cut-out, twelve seconds of ominous silence, and finally the massive explosion.

If that flying bomb really was overhead when its engine cut out there was little hopc of your survival: the force of its explosion was so great that you could be buried alive if your home or workplace or air-raid shelter was inside fifty yards of its impact, and houses would be damaged and windows shattered within the radius of a quarter of a mile.

It was the Blitz all over again, but this time inflicted on a population wearied by five years of war, five years of blackouts and ration books and shortages, of scrimping and saving, making-do and mending; five years of worn-out shoes and clothes, of long queues for food and goods that were basic and limited and not always available. Against such a background, this new onslaught was even harder to bear. We seemed to be like the helpless victims in a terrifying science fiction scenario, struck without warning by implacable weapons from outer space – and applying the traditional British sense of humour by giving them jokey nicknames like buzz bombs and doodlebugs didn't reduce their appalling effect.

The scale of the devastation and demoralisation experienced by Londoners was hushed up at the time, but official papers released long after the war make it clear that it was very serious. By the end of August more than a million people had fled the capital, evacuated either on their own initiative or by the Government. The Tesler family was once again amongst them.

But first there was the little matter of my Matriculation Exam. A letter to parents from the School's new Head, Alan Cooke, optimistically stated that June's General and Higher Schools examinations – today's O and A Levels – would take place "in the Gymnasium as usual"; but the very first day was interrupted by a flying bomb attack, so both examinations were moved lock, stock and barrel to the shelters – how wise their installation now appeared after all – and we finished our week of exam papers underground, accompanied by the sound of droning engines and distant explosions.

It might seem strange to people who have not lived through such a horrendous experience, but in the middle of it all I was never aware of being afraid or feeling that my family or fellow-pupils or teachers or any of the other people I encountered were in fear of their lives. You heard a flying bomb engine cut out and you just dived for cover, never thinking how inadequate that cover might be. In our Watchfield Court flat my mother and sister and I would dive under the kitchen table, which wasn't very big so my mother's rear end would always stick out unprotected – as if that little table could protect anything anyway. We just thought it was funny, not realising how perilous it all was and how lucky we were to be surviving it.

However, my father wasn't taking any chances. He felt that the family would be safer away from London and decided that another evacuation was called for. Luton was a hat-manufacturing town far enough north of the capital to be out of flying bomb range but near enough to be reached fairly quickly by train, and he knew people there who might recommend a suitable boarding-house for us to spend the summer in. So on the last day of the exams, I finished my final paper, said goodbye to friends and teachers and walked home to join my mother and Rosalind in a taxi to Paddington Station, where we met my father and embarked on the early evening train to Luton.

The following weekend a flying bomb destroyed the School cricket pitch, the only section of the playing-field to have remained unspoiled by air-raid shelters; and towards the end of August two more flying bombs fell in quick succession, one on the Girls' tennis court and one a yard or two from the Boys' Hall. They caused great devastation: the Hall was a total wreck, the back wing of the Girls School was very badly damaged, the destruction throughout the entire building was massive; but because it was during the summer break nobody, thank goodness, was hurt.

I can't remember the name of our Luton boarding house, or that of our landlady or the street we lived in for the next few months, but it was all perfectly pleasant, especially for me because I got to know a group of other teenagers, girls as well as boys, who had escaped the air attacks on London with their families. More about my burgeoning social life later, but while we were all serene in the safety of Luton, that summer our air defences were getting to grips with the flying bombs. RAF fighters began to patrol the Channel twenty miles off shore to try to shoot them down before they could reach the south coast; thousands of anti-aircraft guns were moved to the coast as a second line of defence, equipped with the latest in rockets and radar guidance and with proximity fuses on their shells which exploded not only when they hit their target but when they were anywhere near it; behind them was another line of patrolling fighters, and behind that a great concentration of barrage balloons deployed along the North Downs.

By the beginning of September nearly 4,000 doodlebugs – over half of all those aimed at London – had been destroyed before they could reach the capital. In France, Allied air attacks on the missile bases were restricting the number of launches, and as the Allied armies advanced northwards the launching sites began to be abandoned. By early August only twenty-five flying bombs a day were hitting London; by the end of the month only four or five; by the first few days of September all the launching sites had been captured.

In the process, as I discovered to my great surprise in researching this memoir, Allied forces stumbled across another Vengeance Weapon, which would have blown the city to bits if it had been ready before our armies overran the site. This was the highly secret V-3, the so called London Gun: a giant howitzer with a range of 100 miles, its 400-feet long gun-barrel capable of firing three hundred shells an hour at the capital. There were two batteries, each with twenty-five of these monsters, sunk deep into the hill of Mimoyecques in northern France so that all that would be visible from the air were the vents through which their rocket-assisted shells would burst.

Half a century later, Sadam Hussein would be frustrated in his attempts to construct such a supergun to use against Israel; thirty years earlier, in 1914, the Kaiser had actually succeeded in building one and putting it into operation: Big Bertha, Germany's massive World War One howitzer, which demolished Ypres and the French forts at Lieges and Verdun. The London Gun was captured before it could fire a shot, thank God.

By the end of August the flying bomb seemed to have been defeated and thousands of evacuated families returned to London for the beginning of the autumn School term. On September 7 the Home Secretary officially announced the end of evacuation for London; and the minister responsible for coping with the city's flying bomb problem stated that "except possibly for a few last shots the Battle of London is over".

Alas, he couldn't have been more wrong.

Out Of The Frying Pan…

On September 9 there were two mysterious explosions in London, so great that they could be heard all over the city. These explosions continued and increased until by the end of October they averaged four a day. To maintain Londoners' morale and prevent the Germans from knowing the scale of their success, it was two months before the Government admitted that the capital was being hit, devastatingly, by the second of Hitler's Vengeance Weapons, the V-2.

This was the world's first ballistic missile, the work of Germany's brilliant rocket scientist Werner Von Braun, whose ambitions for interplanetary exploration by rocket had been hijacked by the Nazi High Command: when the first V-2 hit London he is reported to have said to his colleagues "the rocket worked perfectly, except for landing on the wrong planet". Von Braun's vile masterpiece was a giant liquid-fuelled rocket-powered bomb with a warhead weighing a ton, launched from camouflaged mobile trailers in Holland. From their launch, these rocket bombs reached an altitude of sixty miles at twice the speed of sound and took only four minutes to reach their target, where they exploded on impact with tremendous force. And their target was London.

The first of the two September 8 bombs fell on Chiswick, outside No 5 Stavely

Road on the corner of the School's Burlington Lane, so there were quite a few boys and girls late for Assembly the next morning. We had joined the throng of awestruck bystanders looking at something that was clearly more than a gas-leak explosion: it had destroyed eleven houses, damaged 600 others in the area and left a crater 40 feet across and 20 feet deep. Miraculously, only three people had been killed.

If the airborne attack on the bridge at Arnhem – the bridge too far – had succeeded and the German armies forced out of Holland, the rocket assembly line buried in the Hartz mountains would have been overrun and the launch trailers destroyed; but the attack went disastrously wrong and London had to suffer another six months of assault from the air – in many ways worse than both the Blitz and the flying bombs.

This time there really was no defence against the unseen enemy: no possibility of interception by day or night fighters, by anti-aircraft fire or barrage balloons; no advance warning – not even the twelve seconds of silence that followed the cut-out of a buzz-bomb engine and gave you a brief moment in which to dive for cover. These vicious weapons struck without warning at any time of day or night; RAF reconnaissance aircraft couldn't spot the mobile camouflaged trailers before the rockets were launched, radar couldn't spot them once they were airborne. By January 1945 they were devastating London at the rate of five a day; for Londoners, the last winter of the war – which coincided with the coldest winter weather in living memory – was the worst.

Ironically, however, although Chiswick had been the very first London suburb to be hit by a V-2, we were spared for most of the rest of that autumn and winter. Unlike the buzz-bombs, the rockets were fired from Holland and so had to pass over Essex and the eastern suburbs to reach central London; the vast majority – and not only those that fell short – landed on the eastern and north-eastern parts of the city, on Ilford and West Ham and Walthamstow (I wonder how Markmanor Avenue fared?), on the heavily built-up working-class areas of Islington, Finsbury and Stepney, and on the old, long-suffering East End.

In Chiswick, while the local authorities did their best to make good the damage caused to Stavely Road by that first V-2 – rebuilding the houses, replacing the gardens, replanting the cherry trees – round the corner in Burlington Lane Mr Dutton and the County School's Sixth Form were busy salvaging the annual School Play. The flying bombs of August had destroyed the Hall and all its stage equipment, but a break in the cherished dramatic tradition was unthinkable. New equipment was brought in, a new stage was improvised in the Gymnasium, which took on the appearance of a charming little intimate theatre – rather like the Q at Kew Bridge

– and the curtain went up on a new production in March 1945.

This was J.B.Priestley's Desert Highway, "a small tribute from a soldier of the last war to the soldiers of this one". It was one of Priestley's "time plays". A British tank crew led by a Jewish sergeant is lost in the Syrian desert and strafed by an enemy plane; the youngest member of the crew dies of his wounds. After the intermission we see a similar group of desert warriors in the same setting in the year 703 B.C., when the Assyrians were invading the Middle East and destroying the peace of the world just as the Nazis did in 1939; once again the youngest member of the group loses his life.

The play drew parallels between the reactions of the two groups to their situation, to war and life and to the death of their comrade. Because of its topicality and Priestley's mastery of character and dialogue, it was both moving and uplifting and the production was a great success. "All the six young actors are entirely satisfying" said the Brentford & Chiswick Times. "The best performance is perhaps that of B.Tesler as the Jewish sergeant. He acts with a quiet sincerity that carries conviction." A Short History of the School notes that the only air-raid siren that sounded during the week's run came a few minutes before the end of the final performance on the Saturday evening. "Not a soul stirred."

Growing Up

Social Life

That previous summer of 1944 in Luton – the flying bomb summer – saw the beginning of my social life as a teenager. I was introduced to a group of young Jewish boys and girls similarly evacuated to Luton with their families, most of them from Wembley; and though they were a little older than my fifteen years we got on well and our friendship continued when we all returned to London at the end of the summer. The experience encouraged me to join the Poplar Grove youth club in Shepherds Bush when we got back home, along with some of my friends from the County School.

Holidays and weekends from that September onwards became pretty full. I was regularly travelling by tube to Wembley or by trolley-bus to Shepherds Bush for parties and concerts. Wembley Town Hall used to hold weekly jam sessions with the best of British jazz musicians. Somewhere in the back of my mind there was always the thought that they might ask a member of the audience on stage to sing with them and I was ready with my version of Sweet Lorraine. I was rather more certain of a performing role at the parties and shows we used to put on for our families and friends in Shepherds Bush.

Poplar Grove's middle-class crowd of personable Jewish youngsters was not so much run as influenced by two very able Jewish matrons: Esther Lawrence, who had been an actress herself and organised our plays and concerts, and Eva Charles, a professional musician who accompanied us on the piano both in the concerts and in the variety shows we put together for ourselves. I have a particularly vivid memory of her accompanying me at a big concert at Tavistock Hall in the West End organised for charity by Lily Montague, doyenne of the Liberal Jewish movement. The performers came from Jewish youth clubs all over London. I sang Louise, a song made famous by a very familiar French entertainer; I was 15: a sort of little Jewish Maurice Chevalier.

Some snapshots – or sound bites – of our variety shows over the next year or two. Mrs Charles's daughter Marie used to sing old music hall songs, and as Maria

Charles went on to be a successful West End actress in revue and comedy; Boris Ashken, son of the local delicatessen owner, gave his impression of Max Miller, complete with white Trilby hat and outrageous floral suits; I sang – usually solo but once, notoriously, with a vocal group made up of three of my County School friends in a medley of Glenn Miller numbers with lots of "doo-wah, doo-wah"s: it took some time to live that down; my friend Jack Samuels and I also developed a music hall cross-talk act – "I say! I say! I say!" – which several years later, performed with fellow undergraduate Colin George, became part of a highly acclaimed University cabaret act: what did they know of music hall who only dreaming spires knew?

One of Mrs Lawrence's productions, Terence Rattigan's Flare Path, was part of a London youth club drama competition and reached the final of a festival of plays performed at Chiswick Town Hall. It came second, but the adjudicator, stage, screen and radio actor Cyril Shaps, awarded a prize for my performance as the Station Officer of a Royal Air Force combat unit, struggling with the personal and professional problems of his pilots and their wives and girlfriends. Forty years later, Cyril Shaps' son Simon worked for me in the features department at LWT, and after a stunning succession of promotions went on to become Director of Television for ITV.

My Glenn Miller-style vocal group was also my own little Watchfield Court Solo School. Like father and mother like son I guess: most Saturday evenings when I was around sixteen, Norman Millar, Barry Levison, Dickie Moore and I used to gather either at my place or round the corner in Wavendon Road at Barry's to play cards, sometimes poker, mostly Solo. Our respective mothers used to prepare biscuits and sandwiches in advance – do people still eat sandwich spread and chocolate spread sandwiches? – and we would make our own tea and coffee and spend the evening talking, joking and playing for pennies.

Dickie was very talented musically; he played baritone saxophone, a fairly unusual instrument for a young lad, and I went along occasionally to hear him with his little group at local dances. Norman was extremely knowledgeable about jazz and moved me on from Glenn Miller and Benny Goodman to Duke Ellington, Bix Beiderbecke and Muggsy Spanier. I began to build up quite a collection of 78 rpm records, guided at first by Norman, who had a huge collection of his own.

That's where my pocket-money mostly went in those days, in weekly visits to the record store on Chiswick High Road – an internet café now – where the attractive female co-owner (another Gwen Dickenson fixation?) used to order my sometimes rather specialised choices from jazz discographies or The Melody Maker – later a rock and roll paper but then a serious journal dedicated to hot music. I remember giving a recital of selections from my record collection to the Youth Club one evening, explaining who was playing what and why I thought it was good or exciting. I think my audience was interested; I know I was. Glenn Miller and Benny Goodman and the other swing bands got me through my School Certificate exams at fifteen; Bix Beiderbecke, Eddie Condon and the Duke got me through Higher Schools two years later. It was Bob Hope movies that got me through my Degree Finals at Oxford, but that's another story.

Another hobby of mine in my mid-teens was photography. We converted the little lavatory at the end of the hall in the flat into a darkroom, where I used to develop and print my own pictures. Like my camera, the equipment was pretty basic, but it worked, and I derived a great deal of fun from it. I'd completely forgotten this particular phase until my memory was jogged by a little trip Audrey and friend Florence Jones and I recently made to Hampton Court Palace – and there, suddenly, were the hugely photogenic stone statues of heraldic animals lining the drive to the Palace entrance, each of which I instantly remembered photographing from every angle on my Sunday morning walks with my father. The home-developing and printing didn't last too long – it was decidedly inconvenient for anyone who wanted to use the darkroom as it was originally intended – but I've never lost my interest in taking photographs.

Like so many youngsters, I was also interested in putting together my own little magazines and comics. I still have a booklet, all in pencil, hand-titled The Winner, noting my address as 44 Markmanor Road and dated 6/5/40 so it was compiled when I was eleven, before the Blitz; in it is meticulously inscribed the Hebrew alphabet and various useful things to remember about Jewish customs and celebrations – inspired no doubt by my weekly sessions with the young visiting rabbi my parents had engaged because I couldn't stand the religion school classes provided by the Boundary Road Synagogue's rabbi, a grumpy old stickler for discipline.

Back in my aircraft spotter days in Holmer Green, I used to make little booklets about aeroplanes – British Fighters Of The Second World War, German Bombers And How To Spot Them, that sort of thing – typing the copy on one of my barmitzvah presents, a portable typewriter, and illustrating it with pictures cut out of Aeroplane and Flight. Now the happy chance that one of my classmates owned a home printing press – his father was a typesetter for a local newspaper – presented me with the opportunity to produce a monthly rival to the School's official end-of-term magazine.

I reckoned that because my publication – The Recorder – would come out more frequently and more quickly than the official one it could be more up-to-date on school events like Sports Day and other fixtures as well as including articles of general interest – well, of interest to me anyway; so I awarded myself the duties of publisher, editor and reporter, commissioned series of articles like The History of Jazz and How To Listen To Classical Music from colleagues, wrote editorials, chased up copy, hunted non-stop for material, ran round on Sports Days desperately trying to keep up with names and events and timings… I stuck it for a year. The experience helped me decades later to appreciate and admire even more the back-breaking work that my son and future daughter-in-law were to embark on with Blitz Magazine and their other publishing ventures.

One of my favourite Sunday morning walks with my father was along the river bank from Richmond to Kew. The river was always an attraction for the family – walks from Strand on the Green to Kew, drives to Teddington Lock, riverboat rides from one of the jetties at Richmond. Sunday morning was also when my father took me back to the East End to buy my clothes and we'd go on from there to visit Booba and Zaida or pop into Blooms for a salt beef lunch.

Odd, the inconsequential little memories triggered in recalling those times: chugging up-river on a brilliantly sunny morning reading The Bishop's Jaegers, one of the marvellously funny books by Thorne Smith, author of Topper; buying my Parlophone Swing Label copy of Benny Goodman's Clarinet a la King from the record-shop next to Blooms; walking out of the gents outfitters in my first – and only – double-breasted sports jacket: I still dream every now and again about those East End menswear shops and the welcome my father always used to receive in them: "*Duvidel! Vuz machs du?*" – roughly translateable as "How's it going, Davey boy?"

A few days after the last night of Desert Highway all German V-2 units were withdrawn from Holland into Germany. There were to be no more air-raids on London, or anywhere else: five weeks later, the Nazi High Command surrendered unconditionally to the Allies. Winston Churchill announced that the war in Europe was over and designated 8 May as Victory in Europe Day – VE Day – a national day of celebration. That day, London, which had undergone so much in bearing the brunt of the German air assaults on Britain, went wild, and that night it seemed as if the entire population of the capital was singing and dancing and cheering in the streets.

The West End was the focus of the celebrations, with Trafalgar Square, Leicester Square and Piccadilly Circus jam-packed with happy, boisterous crowds. It was the biggest, rowdiest, most uproarious party of all time, and my friends and I decided we wanted to take part in it. Public transport had shut down because bus and train drivers and conductors wanted to join in the fun too so we walked all the way to Piccadilly Circus, whooped it up with everybody else, and walked all the way back to Chiswick again. It was very late, and we were footsore and dog-tired, but we knew that we had been part of an extraordinary historic occasion.

My mother had her own way of marking the momentous end of hostilities. She decided that with the war in Europe over she was now released from her patriotic duty, so bacon would no longer be cooked or consumed in the house. Well, you win some, you lose some…

Post-war School

I had done well enough in those air-raid shelter exams of the previous summer for the School to encourage me to take Latin as one of my Higher School subjects as I moved up to the Sixth Form: Latin was an absolute requirement if I was to try for one of the older Universities in due course. That meant getting up to Higher School level in the language from scratch in just two years. I was very fond of Mr Steavenson, the dear old master who taught it. The boys in his other classes behaved abominably to him so it gave me the greatest pleasure to be asked on behalf of the School to make the farewell speech in his honour when he retired.

Last year, after I spoke about my television past at a Royal Television Society Veterans Lunch, the RTS Events Organiser Tony Crabb told me that he'd actually been a younger contemporary of mine at the School and remembered the Mr Steavenson occasion well. He sent me a copy of the School Magazine's report, from which you'll have to forgive me if I quote. "The Captain of the School, Brian Tesler, made what all agreed was a most appropriate and sincere speech, delivered with all the engaging confidence and impressive skill of which Tesler is a real master." Where did it all go?

Thanks to "Stosh" Steavenson, I found Latin as a language pleasingly logical and the myths and legends that informed its history totally fascinating, so the subject wasn't a chore – in fact I got a Distinction at General Schools level, sitting the examination all by myself in the Gym at the end of 1945; and seven months later, in the Higher Schools Exam, I actually got better results in my Latin papers than in my English ones.

By VE Day I was sixteen and half-way through my first year in the Sixth. Charles Garlick, my English lessons guru, thought it might be helpful if I were to visit Oxford in the autumn and have a chat about University prospects with the professor of English at Exeter College, Neville Coghill, who had recently published a much applauded Modern English translation of Chaucer's Canterbury Tales.

The other English don who might have been helpful with advice about college entrance was the equally renowned George Rylands at Cambridge, but we plumped for Oxford because Charles didn't know Rylands as well as he knew Coghill, and I was intrigued by Coghill's theatrical interests – years later he would collaborate in a musical version of the Canterbury Tales in the West End and produce Elizabeth Taylor and Richard Burton (a wartime short-service Oxford graduate) in Marlowe's Dr Faustus at the Oxford Playhouse for a University Charity Gala. As it happens, as an Oxford undergraduate I did meet George Rylands, when I was invited to take an Oxford revue team to Cambridge to provide the cabaret for one of their Summer Balls. I've no idea why they asked us – perhaps the Footlights were performing at another Ball – but it was great fun and a considerable success.

However, all that was in the future; now it was the summer of 1945, the war in Europe was over and, to celebrate, the School decided to combine with Harrow Secondary Grammar to send their senior boys on a field trip to Switzerland. Why Switzerland, why in conjunction with Harrow Grammar, what we would actually be field-tripping *for*, nobody seemed to know, and certainly none of our happy band of combined sixth formers cared to ask: this was a summer holiday abroad – the first in six years for most of us, the first ever for me.

I have a handful of vivid memories of the Harrow and Chiswick School Party trip to set against a general happy haze: our first encounter with Switzerland, changing trains at the terminal at Basle, a vast station gleaming with glass and chrome and, like the rest of the country, spotlessly, antiseptically clean; the coaches waiting for us at Lucerne with banners on their sides welcoming " Mr Harold and Chissy Scoopardy" – I kid you not; the magical day we spent high up on the Great Glaciers – "top of the world, Ma!" – surrounded by ice, snow and mountain peaks under a brilliant blue sky, with the sun hot enough for me to be wearing those Cliftonville white shorts; making my way with friends down the lower slopes of a mountain near the village where we were billeted, down a zig-zag path through the pine trees and bracken, going gradually faster and faster, my momentum increasing as the incline became steeper, the warning cries of my friends growing faint as I realised that the speed of my descent was now uncontrollable, that I wasn't going to be able to take the next zig or zag and would find myself hurtling off the mountainside into God knows what unless I was very, very lucky…

Which I was.

I tripped, grabbed hold of a trailing vine with my left hand as I fell, rocketed over on to my right side and slammed into the bracken, which took the force of my fall. My only casualty was a ripped pair of trousers and a badly grazed leg, which would have been considerably worse if I had been wearing those white shorts. My friends helped me down the rest of the slope and into the village Clinic, where I was treated by a cheerful young doctor for whom my little accident was clearly routine: "Ah! You haff fallen…*up*, yes?" On our coach trip back to the station at the end of our holiday we heard that a Harrow boy had not been so lucky: he'd done the same thing on a different hill and broken his leg.

I had one duty to perform before we returned home. I had promised to bring my father back one of those spectacular automatic Swiss watches that showed not only the time, day and date but the phases of the moon: remember this was 1945 and such state of the art horology could only be dreamed of in war-torn utilitarian Britain. I bought it in Zurich on our last day, and it was a beauty; but it just about cleaned me out: I wouldn't have enough money to pay customs duty on it when we got back to England.

So I'm afraid I committed a crime. I smuggled the watch through Customs. Not only was it a crime; it was a stupid crime: I concealed the watch, wrapped in tissue paper, in my jock strap; and throughout the entire flight home I tried to think how on earth I would explain its presence there if my shifty manner prompted a Customs Officer to conduct a strip search of this obviously suspicious teenage lout. Thankfully it didn't, and I handed over the watch to my father in due course, still warm. Do you think a statute of limitation might apply for this crime, still on my conscience after sixty years?

An Outing To Oxford

My meeting with Nevill Coghill was arranged for late September, just before the undergraduates went up for the beginning of Michaelmas term. My mother, bless her, accompanied me on the train – well, to be correct, my mother took me: what did I know about getting from point A to point B? We arranged to meet for tea at the Copper Kettle in the High after what I was sure would be an ordeal. I'd been invited to lunch with Coghill and the Rector and whichever of the other college dons who might be in residence and curious enough to see this little 16-year old whom Charles Garlick seemed to think was university material.

What on earth was I going to say to them? How was I going to comport myself? I was ushered into the great man's study – big fellow, craggy face, crinkly grey hair, soft Irish accent – and immediately addressed as an equal – "Ah, Mr Tesler, how do you do? I hope your journey wasn't too bad… Chiswick, you say; you know of course that Geoffrey Chaucer lived in Turnham Green: how does the old place look now?... Help yourself to the sherry and we'll join the others in a little while… I understand you've done a bit of acting for Charles; are you interested in that profession or are you cut out for an academic? The last Exeter man who made a name for himself on the stage was John Neville: have you seen any of his work?... Finished your drink? Let's go for a pee and then see what the kitchen has drummed up for us today."

So we went for a pee, and joined the other distinguished gentlemen, and I simply cannot remember anything of what we ate or drank or a single word of what I or anybody else said, not even of when and exactly how we parted company. All I do remember is recovering my consciousness just before I got to the Copper Kettle and thinking that I must have seemed like a speechless, gormless, talentless loon to them all. I didn't tell my mother this, of course. "So how did it go?" "Oh fine, Ma, fine! You know – it was just a little meeting to tell me what University life is like; it was very interesting; yes, it was fine!"

We had our tea and caught the train back to London; and as we sat in our packed compartment, lit only by blue safety lights like the crew of a submerged submarine because Britain was conserving energy as it recovered from the shortages of war, I began to think that my only chance of getting to University was by winning a scholarship. When we got back home I wrote to Neville Coghill, thanked him for our meeting and told him of my intention. He wished me well. Seven years later, in the wonderfully warm letter of congratulation he sent me when I got my degree, I learned what his reaction to that original meeting had actually been: "I knew from the first sight I had of you that you were able, but I thought you might be an idle rogue, possibly even a Smart Alec!" At least he didn't think I was a loon.

Sixth Form Days

I worked very hard in my two years in the Sixth Form, but I appear to have played hard too. I found my School Testimonial the other day, a sort of End of Secondary Schooling Report, signed by Headmaster Alan Cooke in November 1947; and among other things it lists my sporting activities throughout my years in Burlington Lane, including the two in the Sixth, 1945-46 and 1946-47.

I knew of course that I had been part-founder of the School Boxing Club and its Captain in 1946-47 (there really wasn't anybody else to choose from); but I saw to my surprise that I had been in both my House and School Tennis teams in 1946, captained my House in Athletics in 1946 and 1947, and played Cricket for both the House and School 1st XI in 1946 and 1947, captaining the House XI in 1947. All I can actually remember about my sporting prowess, however, is that I could run very fast – on my toes – for short distances, so the 100 yards sprint was my speciality in the field; and on the cricket pitch I could spin the ball prodigiously – I really do mean prodigiously, from leg to off and very nearly back again, as if the ball were controlled by a magnet: the only trouble being I didn't know what I was doing or how on earth I was doing it, and I couldn't do it consistently. Perhaps if we'd had a cricket coach I might have become my generation's Shane Warne. And then again, perhaps not. I see that football wasn't my game, though: according to the Testimonial, I played for my House 2nd XI in 1941-42; and never again.

I was also appointed School Captain in my last year in the Sixth and my teachers were pleased with my academic work so you might think that I was riding pretty high as I got nearer to Examination Week. Not so: I was beginning to lose my nerve. Suppose I failed? What would I do with my life? How would I make a living? My parents could see something was upsetting me and persuaded me to come clean about it. All credit to them, they didn't pour scorn on my fears; they took them perfectly seriously, though they said they had complete confidence in my ability to cope with the exams; and if it didn't work out, said my father, well I could always join him in the millinery trade – perhaps, with my artistic leanings, design hats for Tesler & Fish, and take over the business when he retired: why didn't I come to the office during the Easter break, have a look at what went on and see whether it suited me or not?

So I went to Great Sutton Street and joined my father and my grandfather and the cheerfully welcoming staff, all of them in their white work coats like doctors, on a long factory floor with lines of steam presses, hat blocks and clattering sewing machines, and tables loaded with material and linings, tissue paper and cardboard boxes; and I sat in my father's office and covered sheets of paper with doodled designs for hats – my granddaughters would have loved that – and I thought: who am I kidding? Sorry Dad, but this isn't for me: I'd better stop worrying, listen to a lot more Bix Beiderbecke and Muggsy Spanier and start working really hard on my exam papers.

My parents were quite right. That July, in my Higher Schools Certificate Examination, I achieved a 'Distinction' in History, Latin and French and a 'Good' in English – my best subject! – the equivalent today of an A and three starred A's, for which, to everyone's delight, I was awarded a State Scholarship, which meant that the State would pay for my education at any college whose Common Entrance Exam I was able to pass. What did Charlie Garlick think I should do? "Why not bypass Common Entrance and sit for a couple of Open Scholarships instead – it'll be good experience for you – and ask Exeter if they'll accept you on the strength of your State Scholarship if you don't succeed in pulling one off?"

Why not, indeed? So we looked at various dates and prospectuses, decided on a couple that were conveniently timed at the beginning of the following year, and I wrote to the Rector at Exeter. And the Rector came through: "I note that you will be entering for an Open Scholarship at Christ Church and Jesus. Should you not obtain an Open Award at these colleges we shall be prepared to admit you as a Commoner in view of your State Scholarship."

There was just onc littlc caveat. "Whether we shall be able to admit you in October 1947 or only after your national service it is impossible to say at the present time. The Government regulations about men of your age are not likely to be published until next spring…" So I would have to wait a few more months to know if I would be going up to Oxford, whether as Commoner or Scholar, or heading for two years in one of the Armed Forces.

Two years of military National Service were obligatory in Britain for all male 18-year olds from 1945 to 1963. The war in Europe was over and the war in the Far East ended in September 1945, but Germany and Austria had to be occupied, Palestine policed, Aden and the Suez Canal Zone protected, Cyprus, Singapore, Hong Kong and other British military bases manned, so our depleted, demobbed services had to be augmented by peacetime conscripts, and those conscripts might well include me. Well, I would have plenty to occupy me in the meantime: not just getting myself ready for another round of examinations, but also preparing for my final appearance as a schoolboy actor. "A drum, a drum: Macbeth doth come!"

Macbeth, Part One

The annual School play was produced as usual in the Spring, a double bill of Tobias And The Angel and St Simeon Stylites; but 1946 was a very special year. Chiswick County School had been founded 21 years before in 1925, and to celebrate its coming of age Messrs Kitchen and Garlick planned a spectacular production of Shakespeare's Scottish play – with a cast of 50, the School's most ambitious effort to date. They asked me if I would like to play the lead. I said yes before they'd finished asking the question.

Macbeth began a week of performances on December 9th. I quote the Brentford & Chiswick Times review at some length for two reasons: it was my last appearance as a schoolboy actor and the best notice I ever received as such, and there was a little inadvertent sting in its tail that made me think the theatre was perhaps not where my future lay.

Under the sub-heading A Fine Macbeth it said "The performance of B. Tesler in the title role was first-rate of its kind. He emphasised the finer shades of Macbeth's struggles against evils with a subtlety many a more mature actor could not have excelled. It is not enough that the great soliloquies should be spoken with due regard to their verbal magnificence – as indeed they were – but that they should be accompanied by appropriate gestures. It was a pleasure to watch a young actor who knows how to make every movement significant" – and here's the sting – "A few extra inches would have added to his regal stature, but this was a minor handicap." Minor to you, mate, but to me it indicated that I was not cut out to be an actor in the heroic mould – this was not yet the era of the shorter hero: Al Pacino, Dustin Hoffman, Tom Cruise; if I was going to get into show-business it would have to be by another route.

The review went on to say that "with every desire to pay tribute on which emphasis is rightly laid in school productions, it must be confessed that this Macbeth reigned in rather lonely splendour. And the size of the cast naturally tended to increase his isolation." Too late to make amends, dear reviewer, but thanks anyway. He loved the production itself, the scenery, the lighting and especially the costumes, which were as usual in the hands of the delectable Miss Dickenson: "Costumes were once again something to marvel at in their surmounting of present-day difficulties." Peace-time Britain was still a land of shortages and rationing of clothes as well as of much else, and it couldn't have been easy to dress a cast of 50 convincingly with the resources at Gwen Dickenson's disposal. My crush on Gwen, conceived when I was half her age at 13, had not diminished over the years; now I was a husky (if not heroically tall) teenager of almost 18 and she was only thirteen years older than I. As she dressed and made me up for the final performance that Saturday, was there just the tiniest frisson between us?

Well, a fellow can dream, can't he?

Macbeth, Part Two

Early in the New Year, as planned, I went up to Christ Church and Jesus Colleges and sat their open scholarships, along with dozens of other aspiring youngsters. I remember only two things about that brief sojourn in a bleak, deserted, midwinter Oxford. One is that the weather was viciously cold. One night, in one or other of the colleges, my room was so cold that I couldn't sleep until I had piled my overcoat, a couple of rugs and – believe me – an armchair on top of the totally inadequate blankets on my bed.

The other is my encounter with a fellow aspirant, a year older than I, a tall, thin, gangling Northerner who spoke in a slightly camp Yorkshire accent and waved his arms about a great deal as he did so. Over a drink after dinner in Hall late on our last night, having finished our final exam paper on Shakespeare, a group of us were talking about stage and cinema productions of Shakespeare we had seen and this young man told us that he had directed Shakespeare not only at school but also at the Bradford Playhouse. Not to be outdone, I told him I'd just played Macbeth in a school production which had gone down rather well.

"Do it for me" he said.

"Do what?"

"Something from the play."

"What, here?"

"No, I'll show you where."

So we followed him up the steps from the Buttery, out of the Hall, across the college lawn to what apparently was his staircase, one of the sets of undergraduate rooms to which we scholarship sitters had been assigned. He pushed open the oak door and we stood at the bottom of the staircase itself, which was three flights high with a large window on its top floor landing. "Turn off the light" he said. Someone did, and the staircase and our little group was suddenly lit only by the moon shining through the window at the top of the stairs. "Now, do the Dagger Scene from up there. Start on the landing with the moonlight behind you; let the dagger lead you down to the next landing – that's where Duncan is sleeping. Go!"

So I went: up to the top landing, at midnight, with the moon fitfully lighting the scene, he and the rest of the group looking up at me silhouetted against the window; and I let my imaginary dagger lead me slowly, sickeningly, down the steps to the King's bedroom. "Is this a dagger which I see before me, The handle toward my hand?..." I don't know what it did for the group at the foot of the stairs but there were chills down my own spine, chills I had never felt playing that scene on the stage in Chiswick. This chap really knows what he's doing, I thought; he's got a sense of cinema as well as theatre; and he's only nineteen, damn him!

Four years later he would be directing me in an Oxford University Dramatic Society production of The Duchess Of Malfi at the Oxford Playhouse, with which we would also tour France. Rather more significantly, five years still further on he would be revolutionising British theatre with his production of John Osborne's Look Back In Anger at The Royal Court Theatre for The English Stage Company, which he had co-founded with George Devine, and would go on to make such classic movies as Tom Jones, The Loneliness Of The Long Distance Runner, and The Charge Of The Light Brigade. His name was Tony Richardson.

My Son The Soldier

I failed to win a Scholarship at either St John's or Christ College, as did Tony; and because the legislation on National Service appeared to be confused and contradictory (some occupations were exempt, a shortened length of Service was possible in certain circumstances, the entire period might be reduced to a year for reasons of public economy), I spent a month or so in correspondence with various authorities trying to postpone it until after my degree or obtain an early release from it in order to take up my State Scholarship. Not a chance.

So, having received confirmation from the Rector that my place at Exeter College was secure for October 1949, I resigned myself to a military fate. I received my call-up papers in the summer of 1947 and reported for duty at the Training Depot in Hounslow in October. Hounslow: a short bus-ride away from Chiswick. So near and yet so far: for the entire six weeks of basic training we would not allowed to leave the camp.

They were a gruelling six weeks. All those years ago, for an 18-year old who had never spent a night away from home except on holiday, it was like being thrown into a bath of cold water – almost literally, because Hounslow was a very old camp and its hot-water system was forever breaking down. Fortunately it was a mild autumn, which was particularly welcome if you had to use the loo at night because the loo was a row of out-door open cubicles poised over a latrine trench, with wooden sides and roofs but no doors, wooden or otherwise: I did say Hounslow was a very old camp. With the outside loo in Holmer Green we did at least have privacy, a door and no noxious trench to navigate.

Hounslow squaddies didn't have time to be homesick. We were run off our feet with out-door physical training drill before breakfast, route marches in full uniform, long training runs, weapons drill, parade-ground drill, fatigue duties cleaning up the camp or working in the kitchen – I seemed to be peeling an awful lot of potatoes in those six weeks. We had to spit and polish our shoes, blanco our webbing, iron our shirts, press our uniforms, unmake our beds for daily morning inspection by the sergeant major and officers – "Stand by your beds, you 'orrible lot!" – the sheets and blankets laid out on the mattress, folded meticulously to the prescribed inch – and remake them at night; and try not to fall asleep if at the end of the day we were given night duty as sentries on the overgrown perimeters of the camp. We were treated like incompetent, thick-witted, soft and flabby idiots, and I suppose in the army's terms that's exactly what we were.

Most of us weren't very much different at the end of the six weeks; perhaps a

Dave and Stella.

PICTURE POST

November 1950: my tutors and I make the lead story in Picture Post, the leading illustrated magazine of the time, under the headline "Some of the men who keep the Oxford tradition alive". *Far left,* I'm with Nevill Coghill, discussing the Experimental Theatre Club revue. *Left,* Lord David Cecil.

OUDS tour of The Duchess of Malfi, summer 1951. Nigel Davenport is second from the left; I'm in the centre, and Tony Richardson is to the right, partly concealed

The Girl next Door.

Words and Music by Stanley Myers, Brian Tesler and Julian Dale.

Music of all Music Dealers and of the Copyright Owners—Carolin Music Publishing Co., 3 Soho St., London, W.1.

(Boy.) The girl next door
Is as pretty as paint,
But a heart that's faint
Never won a fair lady,
So I must confess
That I'm no success
With the girl next door.
(Girl.) The boy next door
Is a cute little guy,
But he's much too shy
To even say good morning,
How d'you get to know
A fellow as slow
As the boy next door.
(Boy.) How do you start
A beautiful friendship,
A borrow and lendship
To last all your life?
(Girl.) How do you say to a stranger,
That you'd like to be
His wife for eternity?
(Boy.) The girl next door
Makes me dream all night
Of a future bright,
For two who can live as cheap as one.
(Girl.) I must admit
That I've thought of it
Many times before.
(Boy.) But it wouldn't be fun.
(Girl.) Without the one who lives next door.

(Boy.) The sun was bright,
And she looked so sweet
As down the street
The girl next door came walking,
And I had to say
It's a wonderful day
To the girl next door.
(Girl.) So this is it, well,
I never knew,
What love could do,
But cupid packs a mighty arrow,
Now we've met
I've got to get
That boy next door.
(Boy.) How do you ask
An angel out to dinner?
How do you begin a
Love with just hallo?
(Girl) Wish that I'd learnt about cooking,
Should I ask him round
To open a can or two?
(Boy.) It doesn't matter
What we do,
Our dreams come true
As long as we're together.
(Girl.) We don't care if skies
Are never blue
Or the rain begins to pour.
(Both.) For! *(Boy.)* There'll always be the girl.
(Girl.) There'll always be the boy,
(Both.) There'll always be romance next door.

McGlennon's Song Book, a pre-war publication devoted to the lyrics of the latest popular songs – still going strong in 1950, when it included one of mine. Hard to believe it now, perhaps, but it was good enough for Ted Heath and his Orchestra, Decca Records and BBC Radio at the time. Blame it on my youth…

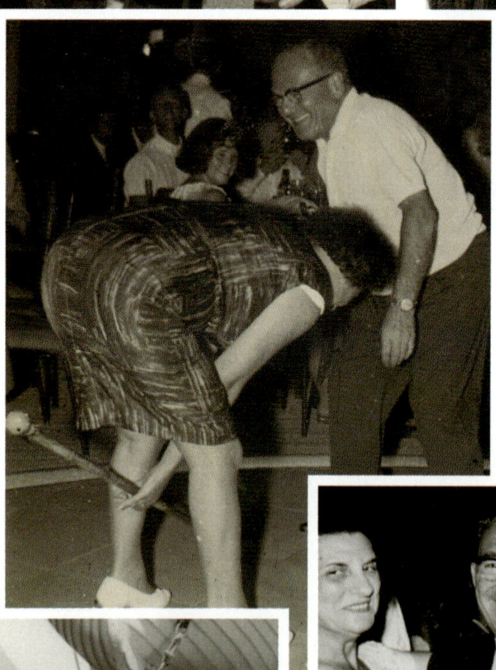

The happy middle years: Dave in the Tesler & Fish white coat *(top left)*; and on holiday with Jean & Maury Levison, Mickey & Shifra Rosenberg and others.

Trading up from our first family car, a Morris Minor, to a Rover saloon.

June 1952: Stella and Dave's Silver Wedding Anniversary. *From left to right at the table:* Uncle Ben & Aunt Betty, Derek and Rosalind; Dave and Stella, Little Booba and me, Cousin Irene and husband Danny Miller, *Behind them, from left:* Uncle Harry and Aunt Annie, a waiter, two family friends, Jean & Maury Levison, Uncle Mick and Aunt Eve, two more family friends, Aunt Pearl and Uncle Sam.

Rosalind's courtship and marriage.

October 1953: the new Mr & Mrs Derek Clayton. In the wedding photograph *(below)* they are accompanied on the left by me, Stella, cousin Denise as maid of honour, and Dave; on the right by Derek's parents, Lily and Jack Cohen.

Audrey and my courtship – in the TV control room – followed in October 1959 by our marriage: accompanied below by Dave, Audrey's parents Vera ('Nana') and Donald ('Bompa'), Stella, Derek and Rosalind.

Cutting the cake with Billy Cotton, Arthur Askey and Eamonn Andrews.

Audrey, pregnant in Yorkshire with her parents and our first puppy, Willie. Simon makes his first appearance *(right)* in November 1961, preceded 18 months earlier by Gary *(below)*.

Dave and Stella with their grandsons *(above)*; and *(right)* with Dave's loyal companion Nikki.

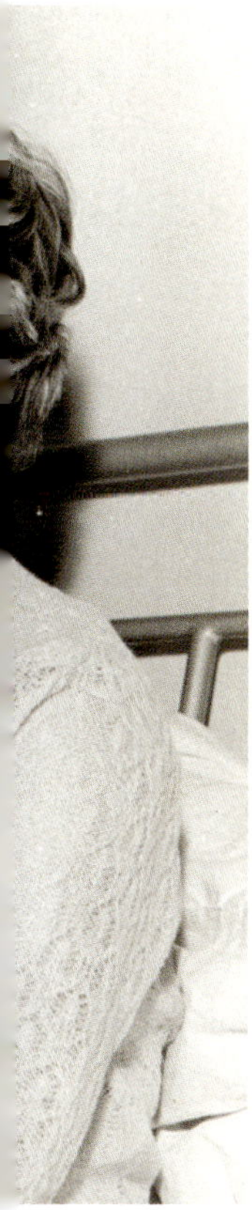

Simon grows up with Willie the Westie.

As a pup, Barkis *(below)* can walk under Nikki's tummy. Before long, Nikki is walking under his.

Stella and Dave

The last picture
of them together,
in January 1972.
He died nine months
later, in September.

Above: four of the sisters - Eve, Betty, Annie and Stella. *Left:* Gary's Barmitzvah in 1973, with Derek's parents. *Below:* Simon's Confirmation in April 1977.

More happy family occasions. *Left:* Simon receives his M.A., Oxford 1982. *Below:* at Buckingham Palace in June 1986 to collect my CBE.

Also in 1986, Stella moves to Homecross House and celebrates with a housewarming tea party. *Above:* with Ben and Betty. *Right:* with Phyllis and Sam.

Stella's 90th Birthday, October 1992. Phyllis gets in first with her speech, and continues to kibbitz, causing me to break up when I attempt my own speech. *Below:* the whole party, except Andrea, who took the picture. *In front:* Phyllis, Stella, Betty. *Behind them:* me, Marise, Rosalind, Denise, Carey, Gary. Back row: Simon, Andrew, Nigel, Jean, Avi, Lindsay, Derek, Audrey, Bernard and Derek.

September 1989: Simon and Carey are married. Stella takes pride of place, along with Carey's grandfather Sydney *(seated left)*, and her parents Sonia and Neville. Seven years later, we are all blessed with the arrival of Simon and Carey's triplet daughters, Nicola, Francesca, and Isabella.

Above: the girls' blessing, in September 1996. Carey's sister Claudia is holding Francesca. The following June, 'Big Grandma' and the girls, toddlers by now, work on their relationship. These are the last pictures of Stella.

September 2001: Gary and Julie are married. *From the top:* Simon, Brian, Audrey, Derek's sister Doreen, Simon (husband of Derek's sister Helen), Helen; Derek's brother Gerald, his wife Jean, Rosalind, Gary, Julie and Derek.

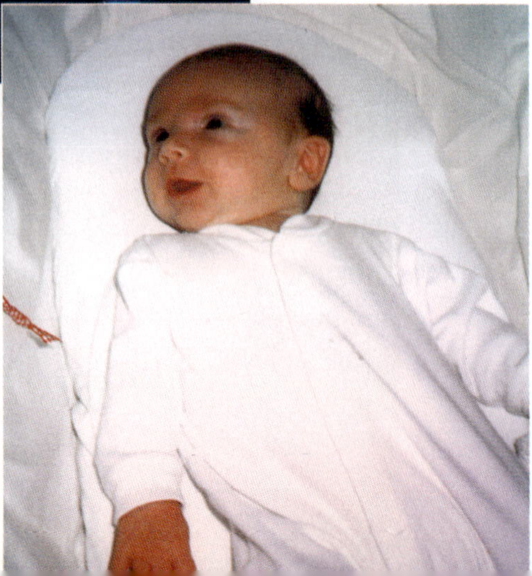

July 2004: a grandson for Rosalind and Derek. Christopher David Clayton, born 27 July 2004, seven weeks after Stella passes away, at the age of 101.

little fitter, a little more disciplined, a little more canny: if you walked about carrying a broom as if you were on your way to fulfil a task, you usually managed to avoid being given one; and the housekeeping skills – sewing, ironing, bed-making, laundering – came into much practical use in my next two postings, though they have long since been lost. The one skill I didn't master was weaponry, so the authorities naturally decided to muster me in the Royal Artillery. I became a Gunner, the Artillery equivalent of Private.

The authorities also decided, rather more sensibly, that I was educated enough to be suitable for office work, so I was drafted to the Artillery Depot at Woolwich to train as a clerk. The Depot was within comfortable striking distance by Tube to the Albert Hall and in the evenings fellow music-lover Gunner Adrian Brown and I made frequent journeys to Kensington to listen to symphony concerts from the topmost reaches of the Hall, where a shilling or two could buy you standing room. During the day, I learned the rudimentaries of filing and how to type quite quickly with two fingers – a skill I have neither lost nor improved upon to this day – and was subsequently despatched to the administrative office of the Royal Artillery base in Rhyl, North Wales: 910112345 Gunner Tesler B., Admin. Clerk, Royal Artillery, reporting for duty, *Sir!*

The duty wasn't very onerous, but it was a pretty tedious life. Office work during the day, a drink and a meal in the Naafi in the evening; Saturday afternoons in Rhyl walking along the promenade, going to a movie, splashing out in a seaside café on egg and chips – my favourite comfort food from way back in Markmanor Avenue – returning to camp on the late bus; Sunday spent in housekeeping chores in the barrack room, washing, ironing, sewing on missing buttons, polishing shoes, listening to the radio.

That's where – ironing my khaki shirts – I first heard a fellow young National Serviceman called Bob Monkhouse in a Forces variety show for new talent. I remember being very impressed by his slick Americanised style, a style I'd grown to enjoy from exposure to all the American comedy shows broadcast by the BBC during the war. Seven years later I would be producing Bob in his own comedy series Fast And Loose for BBC Television and we would become close friends for the next fifty years until he died.

One of the cinemas along the promenade in Rhyl used to show old movies. I remember one Saturday afternoon seeing what appeared to be a 1943 addition to the Dracula saga starring Bela Lugosi, Return Of The Vampire. There I was, sitting almost entirely alone in the auditorium, and there was Lugosi in his familiar role of vampire, but this time he was using what seemed to be Count Dracula's original earthly name: he was introducing himself to the other characters as Dr

Armand Tesler. For one gloriously disorientating moment I thought that perhaps I was descended from a long line of Transylvanian vampires; and seeing the name spelt Armand *Tesla* in the closing credits didn't lessen the impact.

I know now, of course, thanks to Simon's research, that Dr Armand couldn't have been an ancestor of mine: Tesla would have had to be a non-Jewish vampire. I've also learned, via Google, that Return Of The Vampire was a wholesale rip-off by Columbia Pictures of Universal's Dracula movies, retreading the Dracula saga in considerable detail but not daring to use the Dracula name for fear of legal proceedings from Universal Pictures. So they used Tesla instead. Research doesn't reveal why.

My Son The Broadcaster

That apart, together with my brief flurry of boxing activity and even briefer brush with anti-semitism, it was as I say a pretty tedious life; so my heart leapt up when I opened the mail in the Adjutant's office one morning and found a notice for all military personnel inviting them to apply for a post in the British Forces Broadcasting Service. I applied instantly; it took rather longer for me to put the invitation up on the camp's noticeboards : I wanted to get in before any potential competition, I'm still a little ashamed to say.

Within days I was summoned to the BFBS offices in Belgrave Square and interviewed by a Captain Tregellas, who was the spitting image of the monocled, moustachioed man of the world who used to adorn the covers of Esquire magazine. I was shoved behind a microphone for a voice audition, told that I had passed and advised that I would be leaving within a few weeks to join the British Forces Broadcasting station in Trieste, in Northern Italy. Two weeks later, dressed in full army uniform complete with belt, boots and gaiters, my kit bag bulging with books and papers and army gear, I was on the Blue Train out of Waterloo, heading for what would be my home for the rest of my National Service career.

I left a city that, like the country itself, was still deprived, dispirited and down-at-heel after six years of war. Britain was impoverished. If anything, times were harder and life more austere three years after VE Day than they had been in 1945. London was still disfigured with empty bombsites. There were still shortages of housing, of fuel, of goods of every kind. Clothing, meat, bacon, tea, sugar, eggs, butter, cheese, sweets and chocolate were still rationed; even bread, which had been freely available throughout the hostilities, was now on the ration book.

The city I was travelling to had by no means escaped the savagery of war – it was bitterly fought over in the closing months of the conflict by the German army occupying it, the Italian partisans attacking it from the east and the Yugoslav guerrillas attacking from the west. But it had managed to restore itself. I had an intimation of what I would find there in the luxury of the dining car of the train that was taking me down through Europe to the Adriatic: the abundance and variety of food and drink, the apparently unlimited quantities of what was still rationed at home or, if not rationed, simply unavailable. In Trieste there would be the same abundance, the same profusion; I would find a city of bustling trattorias, restaurants and nightclubs, and a relaxed and ample way of life that was totally non-existent back home. It was difficult to comprehend that Italy was technically a defeated nation and Great Britain a victor.

The Villa Triste

Trieste sits at the top of the Adriatic Sea directly opposite Venice, which lies on the other side of the Golfo di Venezia. It was and is a big, beautiful city and an important port, with shipyards, oil refineries and a thriving steel industry: a prize well worth fighting for. The city and the province that surrounded it had been part of the Austro-Hungarian Empire from the 14th century. It had been annexed by Italy after the First World War but now, after World War II, it was being claimed by Yugoslavia, principally on the grounds that outside the city itself the province's population was principally Slav.

Yugoslavia was then very much a part of the Soviet Empire, and the Western allies, wary of the spread of communist power across the continent, firmly resisted its claim; so in 1947, to break the impasse, the United Nations proclaimed a new, independent state for the area, the Free Territory of Trieste. Unfortunately, the UN Security Council couldn't agree on who should govern it, so the Territory was divided in two: Anglo-American Forces occupied Zone A, the Italian-speaking city and its environs; and the Yugoslav army occupied Zone B, the Slavonic-speaking remainder, barbed wire separating the two Zones. Under its leader, Marshal Tito, Yugoslavia refused to follow the Soviet line and in 1948 was in effect expelled from the Soviet Empire, but it was still a communist state and there was great tension between the Zones.

Enter Gunner Tesler.

The Allied Armies were served by two dedicated Broadcasting Services. The American Armed Forces Radio Station had its state-of-the-art studios and control room downtown. The staff of the British Forces Radio Station, set high on a hill overlooking the Adriatic, lived and worked in a beautiful 19th century villa known to the local population as the Villa Triste, the House of Sadness: the Gestapo had commandeered it during the war and our Italian staff were always reluctant to go down to the villa's cellars, where partisan prisoners had been interrogated and, some of them, tortured to death.

The studio centre was more state-of-the-war than state-of-the-art. Our Outside Broadcast equipment was a single ex-BBC ribbon mike, 85 feet of cable and a Ferrograph tape recorder. Our everyday studio was a simple Outside Broadcast van which had slogged its way up Italy through the Italian campaign: a combined studio/control room trailer parked in the villa's magnificent gardens, so that you stepped out of the old drawing room's French windows and climbed a little wooden staircase into the van. A drama and music studio was set up in the old ballroom; and in the attic was a tiny one-man studio for emergencies: the idea being that, if the Yugoslavs invaded and attacked the radio station, one or two of us would lock ourselves in the attic with a pile of gramophone records and a feed to the BBC's Overseas Service, continuing to provide a service for the British Forces, while our fellow broadcasters fought the enemy off with rifles we hadn't touched since we arrived in the city. Well, that was the idea.

Thanks to the vagaries of demobilisation, we were an oddly mixed floating population of Regular Army soldiers and National Servicemen from a variety of regiments and services including the RAF, about a dozen all told: the Station Commander and his Second-in-command, a couple of Sergeants, a Corporal or two and the rest of us other ranks: barely enough to man the station from 6.30 am to midnight in three shifts a day, seven days a week.

There wasn't much time to enjoy all those trattorias, restaurants and nightclubs, which we mostly managed to visit by devising outside broadcasts that would take us there. We lived and worked as civilians, a good deal of the time in civilian clothes: apart from the first few weeks and the odd official visit from military brass – "Ah, so this is where it all happens!" – our uniforms for the most part hung unworn in our wardrobes.

Apart from one of the other new recruits, Johnny Rothwell, who had been a BBC technician, the engineers operating and servicing the equipment were Italian, as were the kitchen and cleaning staff, with whom I got on very well: with my dark skin they thought I looked Sicilian and called me Bruno. There was no more making our own beds or washing and ironing our clothes or cleaning our rooms – although very early on, having annoyed our Regular Army second-in-command by my manner or some military misconduct or other, I was ordered to get down on my hands and knees and scrub the floor of the Reception hall.

Perhaps Neville Coghill was right after all, and I did give the impression of being a cocky young smart alec in need of being taken down a peg or two. I was certainly a few pegs shorter after this indignity, cheered only by the fact that our kindly cleaners, appalled by my humiliation, seized the scrubbing brush and bucket and took over from me as soon as Captain Watkins had moved away.

Whether or not I reformed my manner, for the next twelve months I worked hard and well enough to be promoted when one of our Corporals was demobbed, filling his slot in the station's establishment, my two stripes earning me the rank of Bombardier because I was still officially on the Royal Artillery's muster. And in due course, when it became my turn to be demobbed, the good Captain Watkins would write a glowing testimonial in my Release Certificate. Not only would he praise me as "unquestionably a person of outstanding capabilities and one whose position on the British Forces radio station will be exceptionally difficult to fill"; but also, completely forgetting – or perhaps forgiving – my early floor-scrubbing misdemeanour, he would write under the entry for Military Conduct: "Very Good".

It wasn't difficult to work hard and well in a world that to the boy from Markmanor Avenue obsessed with radio programmes, gramophone records, music, movies and music hall, seemed like living in a dream. When we arrived, of course, none of the National Service recruits knew the first thing about the practicalities of broadcasting: we were just humble listeners. That changed overnight. We were taken into the studio, shown the continuity desk, told "There's the mike. That's how you switch it on. This is what you do to play a record. That's Angelo the technical engineer on the other side of the glass panel – wave back at him, you're going to want him on your side" – and before long we were on our own, apart from Angelo and his colleagues, announcing, presenting, disc-jockeying. And there was I, with a large and well-stocked record library at my disposal, freedom to do any kind of programme I liked as long as it worked, and acres of airtime to fill. Paradise!

Programme Parade

On my study wall hangs a framed collage of cuttings from The Announcer, which was the radio station's Radio Times, and The Betfor Review, a weekly round-up of what was happening in the area under British control – Betfor being the acronym for British Element Trieste Forces. The collage was presented to me in 2003 and I'll explain how and why in another place; but without it I couldn't have remembered the number and variety of the programmes I wrote, produced or presented – mostly all three – nearly sixty years ago.

Quite apart from announcing, linking and disc-jockeying, there were studio interviews, outside broadcast boxing commentaries and a regular two-way Big Band Challenge, with my American Forces Radio counterpart Hal Mansell and me playing rival British and American swing recordings to our combined audiences. Further ransacking the station's record library, there were programmes like Continental Cabaret, goosed up with audience atmosphere and applause to make it sound like the real thing; Dancing Club – "so roll back those carpets and join in!"; and Coffee Time – "Brian Tesler stirs some songs and sequences from the movies into that long second cup of coffee."

There was a regular movie review in Film Weekly; a weekly review of What's On In Trieste; and another of What's On In London for servicemen and women going on leave to or through the capital – courtesy of the magazine What's On In London, which my parents sent me from home every week. There were documentary features like The Story Of Jazz and a series about popular entertainment called Idols And Idolaters, which I hope wasn't as pretentious as it sounds. There was a weekly comedy show, Laugh With Your Luncheon, for which, once I'd exhausted the Spike Jones and Mickey Katz records, the Stanley Holloway monologues and the rest of the comedy material in the library, I wrote the sketches and routines and performed them with John Jacob, Peter Baguley, and Richard Fraser-Harris.

There were chamber music recitals by Trieste's own Quartetto Simini; concerts by the Venezia Guilia Police Band; performances by the Augmented Orchestra of the King's Own Royal Regiment, whose personnel and instruments filled every inch of space in Studio A and spilled into the corridor outside whenever they appeared. I founded the Trieste Rhythm Club and broadcast regular sessions with a swinging little band drawn from both British and American servicemen plus a mysterious Yugoslav called Zeno, who turned up one day and asked if he could play with us. He was one of the finest jazz pianists we'd ever heard, but we never knew his full name or how to get hold of him for a gig; he would just turn up – we suspected from under or over the barbed wire that separated the Yugoslav Zone from ours – and when the session was over he would just disappear again.

Our little swing group also played dances, and I compered outside broadcasts featuring it in settings ranging from Trieste's gorgeous parks to the Army's less than gorgeous barracks and drill halls. We also took our hard-working little OB microphone to Trieste's smart restaurants and nightclubs, where I would give commentaries on the scene and introduce the excellent local orchestras. At one of the nightclubs, the open-air rooftop dance-floor of the glamorous Bastione Fiorito, a tropical thunderstorm broke up the dancing to the Umberto Manzetti Sextet half way through the broadcast; but, rather than return our audience to the studio, I described the chaotic scene while Johnny Rothwell called John Jacob, that evening's station duty announcer, on our field telephone and got him to play records for our listeners to dance to, which I introduced from under a nightclub table hammered by torrential rain.

This adventurous little break from the normal run of radio events appeared to go down well with our listeners, so John and Johnny and I embarked on a series of rather more planned escapades. In one of them, Johnny and I hid in a hillside cave overlooking the city, with a transmitter and a list of records for me to introduce, which John would play back in the studio, and challenged our listeners to find us before the records ran out. A contingent of Military Police managed to run us to earth as if on cue, seven minutes before the programme ended. This particular stunt wasn't repeated, however: the military were not at all amused; every spare jeep in Trieste that evening had been commandeered to scour the hillside to find us.

On another occasion, with the aid of studio sound effects we mocked up a fake aerial tour of the city at night in an open-cockpit bi-plane, with me describing the scene and playing record requests. Suddenly, in the middle of my commentary, we cut the engine effects; Johnny as the pilot, straining to be heard over the wind effects, yelled that the engine had failed. In the fictitious ensuing panic I called out "There's only one thing to do: climb out on the wing and drop in the harbour!", which I proceeded to do – "Good luck, Tesler old man!", "Good luck, yourself old boy!" – bravely continuing with my commentary until it ended in a very large splash; whereupon John, in imperturbable announcer-speak, apologised for the interruption and announced the next record. All of that seemed to us an absolutely obvious gag, but suddenly the studio telephone rang and a crisp voice at the other end of the line said "Captain Roberts here. I've got a launch in the harbour. Can we be of any help?" Maybe Captain Roberts was trying to top us with another gag, but either way it demonstrated our audience's close involvement with the service we were providing.

Socialising

I experienced that audience involvement in a wry way in one of my late-night record programmes. Among the more unusual items in the record library was a set of discs designed to be used by musicians as rhythm-section backing for their practice sessions – a sort of early version of karaoke. The tunes were all standards and the accompaniment first class, so how could I resist? I spent an afternoon with Angelo in the studio, recording my version of some favourite numbers to the backing of these practice discs. I was particularly pleased with one of them – my favourite, Sweet Lorraine – and I played it that night on my Stardust programme, introducing it as a recording by a new singer, Bernie Leigh. I've no idea why I chose that name but I wasn't the only one: years later, on the radio back home, I heard a record by a singer actually called Bernie Leigh; his musical career didn't seem to flourish either.

The recording had barely finished before the studio telephone started to flash. I answered it after my next introduction and heard a warm female voice saying "That wasn't anyone called Bernie Leigh, was it? That was you, and I thought it was great." I had a fan! Her name was Margaret and she said she listened to the station all the time and particularly looked forward to my programmes. We chatted away between record introductions and I asked if she'd like to come up to the Villa one of these days and have a guided tour of the studios. "I'd love to", she said, "How about tomorrow?" Hey! Maybe I had a groupie! Next day, at the appointed time, there I was, eagerly waiting in reception for my guest – and discovered when she arrived that Margaret was not only the wife of one of the King's Own Regiment's officers but she was also ten years older than me, six inches taller, and pregnant. Still, it was a nice visit, and I was happy to dedicate that night's Bernie Leigh special to her.

As it happens, I wouldn't have had the time for a relationship with a fan, let alone a groupie. Social life for station members was severely curtailed. When we weren't working one of the three continuity shifts – 6.30 am to 12 noon, noon to 6 pm, 6 pm to midnight – we were busy researching in the record library; writing our continuity or programme material; rehearsing, presenting or recording our programmes; travelling into town for proof-reading sessions with our Italian printers for The Announcer, or to the British Field Hospital to gather requests for our Hospital Special show; or going out on the road with our outside broadcast unit for Downtown Trieste, in which we talked to servicemen and women at their work and played their record requests.

When we did have some free time, we would take a jeep down to the rocks at Santa Croce for some sea and sun or – courtesy of our American fellow broadcasters – visit the American cinema in the heart of town to see the latest U.S. movies and enjoy the new experience for us of popcorn, Hershey bars and fast food. On one occasion, however, John Jacob and I did manage to spend a weekend's leave across the Gulf in Venice, the first visit to that magnificent city for both of us and perhaps the foundation of John's distinguished future career as museum curator and broadcaster on the arts.

The radio station was also invited to the occasional British or American Services Club function. At one party in our honour, given by the hard-drinking Sergeants of the British Army's Special Investigation Branch, the only clear memory I retain of a long, raucous and very boozy evening is being rolled up in a carpet – I haven't the faintest idea why – to roars of laughter from everyone including myself. Unfortunately I was scheduled to open the station the following day. At 6.25 am next morning, white-faced, bleary-eyed, heavily hung over, I put my head under the cold-water tap in the villa's garden shed to hose myself into some kind of consciousness, staggered into the studio on the dot of 6.30 am to open up the service with a cheery hello to our early morning listeners, put on our stirring signature march and went outside to throw up. I returned to the continuity desk just in time to introduce the first record in our Bright And Early request programme.

Any time I managed to snatch from broadcasting and socialising was beginning to be devoted to study. I needed to get myself into some kind of academic shape for Oxford, to get reacquainted with Eng. Lit., which I had more or less abandoned after the last English paper of my Higher Schools exam. Almost from my arrival in Trieste my parents had sent me the weekly Times Literary Supplement along with What's On. Now, halfway through my posting, I started to ask them for parcels of books I had seen reviewed in the Supplement and thought useful to limber up with: texts and critiques of Chaucer, Shakespeare and the major English poets – I think that's how my series on Idols And Idolaters came about and yes, it probably was as pretentious as it sounds.

My two-year stint as a National Serviceman was scheduled to finish at the end of November, 1949. I had been granted two months' Premature Release to enable me to go up to Oxford in October at the beginning of the Michaelmas Term, plus two weeks of Release Leave, so in the middle of September I said goodbye to Trieste, to the station, the staff and my colleagues; and clad once again but for the last time in uniform, I was sent back to Britain by troopship. I took the train to the Royal Artillery depot at Aldershot, and there, on 15 September 1949, I was demobbed from the Army at last.

I had had a hugely rewarding time at the radio station and in many ways I was sorry to leave. Ian Woolf, the Station Commander, tried to persuade me to stay on as a civilian broadcaster and I confess that I was tempted, but I couldn't possibly throw away the opportunity that my State Scholarship had given me. And perhaps I would get back into broadcasting some day: after all, David Watkins's generous Testimonial did say "I have no hesitation whatsoever in most strongly recommending him for any job similar to the one he has been doing here", which might open a door for me somewhere, some time.

Three years later I would indeed be doing a similar job, though in television not radio; and twenty-five years later, in 1974, Ian Woolf's path and mine would cross again. By then, Ian had become the Director of Forces Broadcasting and I was John Freeman's Deputy Chief Executive at London Weekend Television. LWT had won the contract to transmit the daily television schedules of the British Forces Broadcasting Service to their transmitter in Celle, West Germany, for onward transmission to the barracks and homes of the British Army of the Rhine, and I was invited onto the BFBS Board as a sort of liaison officer. Three years later, the BBC pulled out all its previously complacent stops and won the contract from us, but BFBS asked me to stay on the Board as a non-executive director, which I did for the next 25 years, seeing them through their merger with the Services Kinema Corporation to form the Services Sound and Vision Corporation, and long past Ian's retirement. It was when I myself retired from the Board, in 2003, that I was presented with that collage of cuttings from The Announcer.

But now, at the age of 20, after two hectic weeks at home in Chiswick with family and friends, I was on my way to Exeter College with my books, my luggage and my little sherry set of decanter and glasses without which, so I understood, social life at Oxford was inconceivable. They tell me that sherry is not so big in undergraduate circles today…

What Happened Next?

Fast-forwarding...

What happened next was the rest of my adult life: fifty-seven years of it at the time of writing, forty-two of them spent in television. They would take up the pages of a very much larger memoir than this, but I ought to tackle it some time: my professional career did after all encompass the entire evolution of post-war British television from a single-channel BBC to today's explosion of satellite and cable channels, and it would be a pity not to record something of my experience of it.

My life in television began in 1952 as a trainee producer at the BBC and ended as Chairman and Managing Director of London Weekend Television. As a producer, I was the first winner of BAFTA's Light Entertainment Production Award. As an executive, I was Director of Programmes for ABC Television and Thames Television; a founder-director of Thames Television and Channel Four; the founder-Chairman of both ITV's first Teletext company, Oracle, and ITV's first venture into satellite broadcasting, ITV Superchannel. I worked for four legendary broadcasting bosses: Ronnie Waldman, Lew Grade, Howard Thomas and John Freeman; and when I was a broadcasting boss myself at LWT I appointed three future legends successively as my Director of Programmes: Michael Grade, John Birt and Greg Dyke. So there is an abundance of things to record – decades of people and programmes, confrontations and negotiations, alarums and excursions, good times, bad times...

I didn't write anything down during those years either.

Other people did, however. I make an appearance, in roles ranging from walk-on to lead, in numerous books about British television: for instance, in the autobiographies of Howard Thomas, Bill Cotton, Michael Grade, Jeremy Isaacs, John Birt and Greg Dyke; in volumes two to six of the official history of ITV, Independent Television In Britain; in David Docherty's history of LWT, Running The Show; and in Mark Lewisohn's encyclopaedic Guide To TV Comedy. There are recollections and tributes from broadcasting friends and colleagues in the massive album presented to me on my retirement from LWT. I also have correspondence, programmes and press cuttings to evoke my three years at Oxford, much of which was spent writing, producing and performing in plays, revues and cabaret with such now celebrated names as John Schlesinger, Michael Codron, Nigel Davenport, John Wood, Maggie Smith, Stanley Myers and Tony Richardson; although, inspired by my tutors Neville Coghill and Lord David Cecil and the infinite splendours of English language and literature, I did enough work to gain a First Class Honours degree.

So perhaps it wouldn't be too formidable a task to jog my memory and move the story on, though it would certainly be time consuming. Meanwhile, this part of the story is very much less than complete. I began Before I Forget in order to capture memories of my family, and there are many more of those memories to come.

Back To The Family

Stella and Dave celebrated their Silver Wedding in June, 1952. The photograph of the family and their friends sitting or standing round the dinner table "before the off" as my father would have said, is rare indeed: all the Hyman girls and their husbands are there, all together in the same setting: Annie and Harry (the only picture I ever remember seeing of Harry), Betty and Ben, Eve and Mick, Pearl and Sam – Sam towering over everybody else – with Stella and Dave seated in the middle of the group behind the flowery table centrepiece.

Of the rest of the family, there's Rosalind, with her dashing young boyfriend Derek, to the left of Stella and Dave; over on the right, there's recently married cousin Irene with her husband Danny. The other cousins are too young for a grown-up black-tie do. For some reason cousin Willie, the oldest of us all, is missing too. (He had also by now adopted the more adult first name of Sam, and changed his surname to Kelsey.) There am I next to Stella and Dave with my five o'clock shadow, still wondering what kind of degree I am going to receive that summer. And there, seated between my mother and me, is the tiny figure of Little Booba.

Little Booba – Grandma Yetta – had outlived both my other grandparents. Grandma Sophie – Big Booba – died in December 1947 and Zaida – Grandpa Gershon – in February 1950. We know from his death certificate that Zaida was 73; Sophie probably wasn't even 70. Yetta must have been in her late 70s or early 80s at the time of the Silver Wedding photo. She died not much more than a year after that happiest of occasions and was buried from her house in Markmanor Avenue, from which neither the Blitz nor anything else had previously managed to move her.

The '50s were good years for my parents. Rosalind married Derek in 1953 (don't think of it as losing a daughter, Stella and Dave: think of it as gaining a bedroom for your son). The son became a successful television producer and was financially off their hands though not yet out of their flat. Dear Mr Fish had died in the late '40s but Tesler & Fish (Dad kept the company's name) were still doing well although the war had radically changed women's hat-wearing habits and the millinery business would never regain the dizzying heights of the '20s and '30s. Stella and Dave were free to enjoy themselves with their many friends, at card parties and social gatherings, at family get-togethers, on holidays at home and on the continent, and on international cruises.

My father was a dedicated Freemason and had become the Worshipful Master of his Lodge, so Lodge Meetings took up quite a bit of his time, as they did for my mother, who joined a women's Lodge and became an equally gregarious lady Mason, or Maisonette as jolly male Masons liked to call their counterparts. Puffed by the hour-long walk it took to get to the Brook Green Synagogue in Hammersmith on Saturday mornings and High Holydays, Dad clubbed together with his friends, rented a house in Barrowgate Road and started up a local Synagogue for the good Jewish burghers of Chiswick and district. And there was always the allotment.

Both my parents were tickled pink by my success in television, my father especially: it was a great help in his running game of one-upmanship with Jack Lyons, whose carpet business occupied the factory floor above his in Great Sutton Street. By the middle of the 50s, and particularly with the advent of ITV, television was front page news in all the newspapers – not just every little off-beat incident in the live programmes that went out each night but also gossip about the comings and goings between channels of performers and writers and even producers.

When I left the BBC to join ATV at the end of 1956 there were little paragraphs about my departure and the salary for which I was allegedly leaving: £10,000 said the Daily Telegraph, which was about three times the actual figure. My father was particularly pleased with himself when he came home for dinner that evening. Apparently everybody he'd seen that day had congratulated him on his son's success, including Jack Lyons. "You didn't tell him the salary in the Telegraph was right, did you, Dad?" "No, of course not" he said. "But I didn't tell him it was wrong, either."

Three years later, when I moved from ATV to ABC as an executive, the newspapers quoted my new salary as £5,000, which happened to be the correct figure; but how was my father going to handle the apparent drop in salary with Jack Lyons? "What did Jack Lyons say, Dad?" "He said 'So tell me, Dave: your son's new job, it's a promotion, yes ?'; I said 'Yes, of course'; and he said 'But Dave, if it's a promotion and he was getting £10,000 a year for the old job, how come he's only getting £5000 a year for the new one?'; and I said 'Ah, that's *as well*'!"

Early on in my first year at ATV, I began to notice the young Production Assistant who worked along the corridor for a fellow light entertainment producer named Albert Locke. Her name was Audrey Maclean; she was blonde and bright and extremely attractive; and increasingly I would find myself wandering into Albert's office, often several times a day, to ask his advice about something or other and in passing, naturally enough, having a word or two with this beguiling young woman: I must have been under the spell of the pretty green dress with yellow flowers she often wore and which I still remember nearly fifty years later. Sometimes I was lucky enough to find Albert absent, so I could chat to Audrey without having to drum up an idiotic excuse; and that summer I was luckier still: my Production Assistant had to change her holiday dates just before a Johnnie Ray Spectacular I was scheduled to produce. Albert didn't have a show of his own to work on, so Audrey was assigned to my show instead.

As possible bookings for the Johnnie Ray production, the Grade agency asked me to have a look at some international speciality acts who were playing in that season's Summer Shows in Great Yarmouth; so before rehearsals began Audrey and I took a trip to the coast to check them out. We saw the shows, booked one of the acts, stayed overnight in a hotel – separate rooms of course – and drove back to London after a long, sunny, chatty walk along the promenade. The attraction appeared to be mutual; the Yarmouth expedition had been an ideal opportunity to get to know each other; and in the Johnnie Ray rehearsals the following week we found that we worked well together as a team. By the time the show was over we were, as they say, an item. At the beginning of the autumn schedule, ATV agreed to make Audrey my P.A. on a permanent basis, Audrey bade her fond farewells to Albert Locke, and she and I embarked on a partnership that has in all lasted forty-nine marvellous years to date and still counting.

We married on October 28th 1959 at Caxton Hall, choking with suppressed laughter because the Registrar had a twisty, whiny voice like Pa Kettle in the Ma and Pa Kettle movies. The wedding reception was at the Washington Hotel in Curzon Street and the photographs don't really resolve the happy blur of that occasion. ATV's house photographers were covering it, and they tended to concentrate on the stars who were present, people like Eamonn Andrews, Billy Cotton, Arthur Askey, Dave King, Jack Parnell and Roy Castle, so the pictures don't give us many clues as to who else was there. But they couldn't of course avoid taking shots of my parents and Rosalind and Derek, Audrey's parents Vera and Donald (known to us and everybody else as Nana and Bompa) and Audrey's sister

Pym and husband Ian Carmichael – another star for the cameras to home in on – together with their daughters Lee and Sally; but there are good sightings of my parents' friends and some of mine, and of Audrey's friends and other members of her family; there's a glimpse of cousin Derek in the background of one shot and Denise's little sister Lindsay in another, so Betty and Ben and their son Nigel must have been there too.

Unfortunately, Denise herself wasn't present: she was expecting her own happy event, the imminent birth of her son Roland, or she would probably be able to trot out the entire cast; but I can't imagine any of the other aunts and uncles and cousins missing the event – except, alas, for the Levingers. Uncle Sam had died earlier in the '50s. After that sad event Pearl had joined her daughter Irene in America, Irene having divorced her first husband and married the actor Martin Balsam, and Hilary had married and made her home in Australia, so that branch of the Hyman clan was unfortunately missing from this happy family occasion.

Another Tesler Family Begins

Audrey and I moved into a basement flat in Knightsbridge with our first little puppy, a pedigree West Highland terrier officially named Junyer Johnnie of Sussex but rapidly renamed Willie the Widdler – Willie for short – because that's what he was really good at, swiftly christening the carpet of our new home and the carpets of several of our friends before we were able to train him otherwise. Our flat was the basement of number 15 Ennismore Gardens and the house next door but one was numbered 12a rather than 13, presumably for superstition's sake. Both houses, together with number 14 in between, belonged to Lord Chesham – our dustbins proudly proclaimed the name CHESHAM in large white letters – and the wall between the first floors of 12a and No 14 next door to us had been removed to make a single large first floor apartment.

As it happened, Lord Chesham was the uncle of a young television director, Kim Mills, whom we had only recently met and who became a close and dear friend of ours, but that was only a minor coincidence. The major coincidence was that, a year after we moved into number 15, another young married couple moved into the first floor flat that ran across both No 12a and No 14. They were Sonia and Neville Labovitch, to whom, oddly enough, we were never introduced although both we and they knew the couple who lived on the ground floor of our house, John and Joan Golfar. Sonia and Neville were accompanied by their baby daughter Carey. So when our son Simon was conceived, and while he was quietly gestating in the basement of number 15, his future wife was sleeping peacefully in her cot next door two floors above him. I don't know about you, dear reader, but as coincidences go, that seems to me to be a lulu.

Simon was born on November 1st 1961. He was a beautiful and brilliant baby and, sparing his blushes, he has remained beautiful and brilliant ever since. I'm essentially a company man, someone who has only ever worked for one big organisation or another, so I have the greatest admiration for my son, who has achieved success as his own boss, working essentially for himself or, in their hectic magazine years, alongside Carey; but I'm not going to go into Simon's story in this memoir: that's for him to do in his own way, in his own time, for his own grandchildren – though I hope that, unlike his father, he is writing things down in the meanwhile.

I will only say that in all these years, with the exception of a brief period of teenage rebellion – watch out, Simon, you've got three of those yourself coming up in due course – he has given Audrey and me nothing but joy and happiness, especially, in September 1989, in marrying the equally brilliant and even more beautiful Carey, and in the two of them, in March 1996, crowning our lives by producing Nicola, Francesca and Isabella, who have taken beauty and brilliance to a level undreamt of in Markmanor Avenue.

We had never intended the basement in Ennismore Gardens to be our permanent home: it was hardly big enough for the two of us and Willie so it certainly couldn't have accommodated the family we hoped for as well. During most of 1960 and into the early months of 1961 Audrey went hunting for a bigger flat or a cosy little house somewhere in London, with me taking time out from the ABC Television studios in Teddington, where I had taken up my first programme executive position, whenever she thought there was something promising for me to look at. And when at last she became pregnant, Audrey started to take religious instruction at the Liberal Jewish Synagogue in St John's Wood with the intention of converting to Judaism before Simon made his entrance. It would be a close-run race.

Audrey came from good, solid Protestant stock, although she was no more religiously orthodox than I was. We both felt that Simon should be born into his father's faith, whatever he might ultimately choose to follow, and Liberal Judaism's philosophy and ideals, while deeply rooted in classical Judaism, seemed particularly well suited to life in 20th Century Britain. I had long ago left the Orthodox Synagogue, deterred among other things by the fact that its services were conducted entirely in Hebrew and the male and female members of its congregations were separated so that families couldn't worship together.

Reading Audrey's books and discussing her essays and lessons with her brought me back to the religion again, not least because the Liberal Jewish service is conducted in English as well as Hebrew and the male and female members of its congregations do worship together. The service certainly impressed my parents when in due course we took them to St John's Wood. Accustomed as they were only to the practice of the Orthodox synagogue, they listened to the beautiful sound of the choir and the happy participation of the male and female worshippers around them and, understanding perhaps for the very first time what an officiating rabbi was actually saying, my mother leaned towards me and whispered "It's marvellous, darling. They should do this in *Jewish* synagogues as well!"

Audrey passed her examination with flying colours and we were married again in a religious ceremony at St John's Wood. No suppressed giggles this time, and she was no longer pregnant: Simon was already sleeping in his little cot in our new home. Audrey had looked for it all over North and West London. There hadn't been much in the price range we had set ourselves and Chiswick wasn't anywhere near the top of the list of areas we fancied, but in the end we settled for a family house in Park Road, a few doors away from the entrance to Chiswick House through which I had last walked to school fourteen years before; and we moved in just before Simon was born.

The strange thing was that from the moment we took out the mortgage on Park Road I stopped having a recurring dream that had haunted me night after night for many months. The dream was by no means an unwelcome one. It invariably found me walking through a long green tunnel suffused with light, feeling both happy and at peace. It was a dream I was sorry to lose – the dreams of television executives are not often happy and peaceful – and I couldn't imagine why it should stop, as suddenly as it had started. Until six months later, in our first summer in Park Road…

Willie and I had gone for an early walk in the grounds of Chiswick House before I was due to leave for the studio. It was a gloriously sunny day, and as we made our way through the park gate and along the path leading to the classic bridge I suddenly realised that we were in fact walking through my dream: the foliage of the trees lining both sides of the path had interlaced to form a roof and the sun was pouring through the leaves, turning the path, the trees that lined it and the roof itself into a long green tunnel of suffused light.

And of course that was the way it must have looked when I walked to school all those happy, halcyon summers ago. Having used the dream to point me in the right direction, my subconscious clearly felt that I didn't need it any more and it has never returned. I was home; and Park Road has remained home ever since.

A Change Of Life

Driving back from his factory on the evening of 19 January 1966, my father felt a severe pain in his side. He thought it was a stitch and stopped the car to get out and stretch his legs to ease it. The little walkabout didn't help: indeed, the pain grew worse; but he managed to get back into his car and crawl home. As soon as Stella saw him she rang for an ambulance; Dave was rushed to the Royal Masonic Hospital in Ravenscourt Park and straight into the intensive care unit. He had suffered an aneurism of the aorta: the wall of the main artery to his heart had ballooned; if it had burst, he would have died on the spot, and the possibility of that happening was still very real. The stress of years of driving to and from his factory across London in the rush hour had finally been too much for someone with high blood pressure who had smoked up to forty cigarettes a day for most of his adult life: pretty well a textbook case and almost always fatal.

Miraculously, the aorta didn't burst.

Rosalind had started to keep a diary at the beginning of the year, so we know in some detail what Dave went through during the next few months. He was kept in intensive care for a week under heavy sedation, restless and hallucinatory, strapped to his bed so that he couldn't move, while the doctors pumped drugs into him to reduce the pressure on the wall of his aorta and bring the ballooning down. It was another fortnight before they considered it safe enough to move him to the specialist care of a teaching hospital, and on 4 February he was transferred to St Mary's in Paddington.

After two more weeks, the crisis was deemed to be over and he was sent back to the Royal Masonic Hospital to begin the slow road to recovery; but calamity hadn't finished with him. The night before he was due to return to the Masonic, on 16 February, a fire started in Jack Lyons's factory on the floor above Tesler & Fish in Great Sutton Street. It quickly spread to Dave's own floor and both factories were consumed by the flames before the Fire Brigade could get the blaze under control. Dave's factory was ravaged: the machines and blocks, the bales of material, the finished and unfinished stock, were all destroyed or irreparably damaged. It would cost a fortune to reinstate; and, as we were to discover, that fortune was not going to come from the insurance company: Dave was inadequately insured. He was ruined. His business, quite literally, had gone up in flames.

These were only the early stages of his recovery so there was still the risk of a relapse and the doctors asked us not to tell him about the fire. This wasn't at all easy because as he improved he naturally wanted to know how the business was doing in his absence. He kept asking us for news, and we kept telling him that everything appeared to be fine. His manager, whose nickname I remember was Dolly, came to see him as soon as it was possible for Dave to have visitors other than close family, but he made the mistake of doing so on a weekday. Although Dave was glad to see him and to have an opportunity to ask what was happening in Great Sutton Street, he couldn't understand how Dolly could leave the factory in the middle of the week: "Who's looking after the business?" The poor man improvised some story or other but he was no more convincing than Stella, Rosalind or I had been; and I'm pretty certain that my father suspected something was wrong long before we actually told him.

At the beginning of March, with his nurse's help, Dave was able to get out of bed and walk round the ward. A week later, when it was thought he was strong enough, I broke the news to him; and, to my surprise, after the initial shock he was remarkably philosophical about it. "Look, son, I'm lucky to be alive. The doctors tell me I've got to take it easy, I mustn't drive, I shouldn't go back to work again… and now I couldn't go back to work even if I wanted to. So I'll retire. I'm 65 next month – I'll be a full-time old-age pensioner!" On 11 March Dave was sent home. He had been in hospital for just under three months.

As it turned out, life as a full-time pensioner wasn't all that bad: Jack Lyons's fire was something of a bizarre blessing in disguise. The aneurism and its aftermath had knocked the physical stuffing out of Dave. He needed a long, slow convalescence and once his affairs were wound up and his manager and staff had been looked after as well as possible, it was a relief to be out of the rat race, free of the stress of running a business in an industry that was increasingly on the decline.

Dave had enough money for himself and Stella to live on – a little more modestly than before, perhaps, but comfortably enough. They still had their friends and their holidays, though for health's sake there would be no more flying, no more overseas trips: it would be back to Bournemouth again. And they had their family as the most agreeable of preoccupations: Rosalind and Derek had given them their first grandson, Gary, eighteen months before Simon was born, and the two boys were an unfailing delight for their grandparents, whom they saw every weekend.

They also had a new part-time vocation. Whenever Audrey and I went away for a January holiday in the sun, Dave and Stella would come and live in our house and, with our au pair's help, look after both the house and Simon. Apparently Simon sometimes took quite a bit of looking after: one January, when he was seven years old, the only entry for the entire month in the diary he had been given the previous Christmas was "Grandpa got mad!"

At other times of the year – in the summer, when we'd take Simon with us to

Yorkshire and our au pair would go off on her own holiday, or at Easter or in the autumn or often both, when we'd take Simon together with the au pair up to Yorkshire – Dave and Stella would look after the house by themselves and have their friends over to Park Road for their card-evenings.

Our Yorkshire trips were to Audrey's parents, who still lived in the family house where Audrey was born, near Whitby, in the little village of Sleights, in the parish – as I never cease to love rolling off my tongue – of Eskdaleside-cum-Ugglebarnby. Dear Vera and Donald, Nana and Bompa: a lovely, down to earth couple with a fascinating background – Nana from a long line of sea-faring captains and Bompa, member of the Maclean clan and the Pyman shipping-line dynasty, who had seen active service in both World Wars... Audrey should do her own family memoir, though it's more than likely that nobody has written anything down about the Maclean/Clark story either.

Those were idyllic holidays for Simon and Audrey and me, which none of us will forget: clambering up Battle Bank; walking through the woods between Falling Foss and Littlebeck; wading down the stream that twisted and turned at the bottom of Bompa's poultry farm until it joined the river Esk; delicately handling the farm's little chicks and Billy Bantam, its prize rooster; swimming at Sandsend; watching the fishing-boats in Whitby Harbour and the steam trains rattling through Sleights station; climbing the hundred-and-one steps to Whitby Abbey; hunting for crabs at Robin Hood's Bay when the tide was out; boating on the river at Ruswarp; navigating the stepping-stones at Darnholm and the goats at Goathland...happy, golden days.

The Days Dwindle Down...

Back home in Chiswick for Dave there was a new hobby: dog-walking. Willie the Westie died in 1967 at the age of eight, and he was succeeded by a miniature schnautzer who was also of pedigree stock, with the kennel name of Deltone Delaunay – we called him Nikki, which better fitted his boisterous personality. He was a handsome, friendly little fellow, and Dave fell in love with him at first sight. The feeling was very much reciprocated; and on dry, clear days, Dave would take a leisurely walk from Watchfield Court to Park Road – retracing the route the family had taken twenty-five years earlier on its very first day in Chiswick – to take Nikki into Chiswick House for his mid-morning exercise. This would be followed by a cup of coffee and a little chin-wag with Audrey, and then Dave would walk back to Watchfield Court for one of Stella's delicious lunches.

Not a bad way to spend a morning.

Dave and Stella enjoyed six more years of this happy retirement; and then on 4 June 1972 Dave suffered a mild coronary attack, which took him back into the Royal Masonic Hospital. He was discharged after only a week, but the attack had shaken his self-confidence and he was never quite the same again: a little more subdued, a little less ebullient – and the dog-walking became a little less frequent. Earlier that year at a dinner-party, Audrey and I had fallen for another little puppy, the runt of a litter resulting from the brief encounter of our host's Alsatian bitch with a passing Labrador. All the other puppies had found a home, but not this poor little fellow. It was too much for sentimental dog-lovers like us to bear, so we offered to take him back to our home, where he could be a friend for Nikki and another walking-companion for Dave.

And so it had proved. Like us, Dave had fallen for Barkis – we named him after the Dickens character because he was such a willing little chap – and he was more than happy to include him in their Chiswick House rambles. But by the time Dave came out of hospital after his coronary, Barkis had grown into a large and floppy young bouncer, who liked to express his affection by jumping up to land great wet licks on everybody he loved. Even though the affection was shared, this was more than Dave could now cope with, so the dog-walking was not only less frequent but increasingly without Barkis, who began to find himself, puzzled and at a loss, left behind in the garden.

On the first Sunday in September of that year, Audrey and Simon and I collected Stella and Dave and we all drove over to Edgware for tea with Rosalind and Derek and Gary. It was a delightful little family gathering, as always. Five days later, on 8 September, Stella and Dave finished their breakfast in the kitchen at Watchfield Court and Stella went to the sink to start the washing up. They continued cheerfully chatting away until Stella asked a question to which Dave didn't reply. She turned round to repeat it, and saw Dave slumped forward, with his head resting on the kitchen table. He had died, instantly, from a massive heart attack.

My father was 71. It had been a long journey from the little Russian village to a fashionable West London suburb but he had accomplished it with style, ending up as a proud Englishman, a successful man of business, the founder of a synagogue, the Worshipful Master of a Masonic Lodge, the life and soul of a large circle of friends. When I think of my father – and something reminds me of him almost daily – I remember an amiable, gregarious, loving family man, with a great sense of humour and an endearing affection for show business.

There seems to be more of him in me each day, whether genetically or by unconscious imitation – certain mannerisms, particular turns of phrase, the involuntary little cough; and, as Audrey is only too aware, I frequently find myself repeating his jokes and punchlines. But I owe him much more than that. What would my chances of a university career have been if he had not uprooted himself and his family from the other side of London so that I could return to Chiswick with the County School? And in which direction would my professional career have gone without the music-hall, music, movies and theatre to which he exposed me in my childhood and youth?

Stella, Alone

My father's death hit Stella hard but, indomitable lady that she was, she pulled herself together and set about living life for one at Watchfield Court. She had a sizeable circle of friends in the flats and kept in touch with all the friends she had shared with Dave; and before very long she was going on cruises and seaside holidays with them again. Most weekends she spent with Audrey, Simon and me in Park Road or with Rosalind, Derek and Gary in Edgware, sometimes with all of us together at one or other of our homes. From time to time there were still the Festival night dinners at Watchfield Court with Stella, the traditional Yiddishe Momma, cooking and serving – and hovering while the rest of us ate her gefilte fish and chicken soup. She extended her catering expertise to the Christmas lunches Audrey and I used to give to the heads of my programme department at Thames, to which she contributed her delicious fruit pies as well as her presence; and she radiantly enjoyed her matriarchal status at the family's happy occasions – Gary's barmitzvah in 1976, Simon's confirmation in 1977, my CBE in 1986, Simon and Carey's joyous wedding in 1989 – and those of her sisters and their families.

There were, alas, less happy occasions to attend as well. The days were also dwindling down for some of the other Hyman Girls. There's a happy photograph of four of the sisters in 1963, in the garden at Park Road. It's a sunny summer's day and Eve, Betty, Annie and Stella have been picking plums from our plum tree; only Pearl, still in the States, is absent. Sadly, in 1965, two years after the photograph, Eve died; she was followed a year later by Pearl and in 1970 by Eve's husband Mick. Poor cousin Derek and the Chason branch of the family: having lost his mother and father, Derek was hit by further disaster in 1978 when his wife Penny died, tragically young.

By the spring of 1986, Watchfield Court was more than Stella could manage by herself, and on the first of April we moved her out of the family home in which she had lived for 44 years to a pretty little flat in Homecross House, a sheltered accommodation development on the other side of Chiswick High Road, where she would continue to cook and clean and look after herself for the next nine years. To mark the occasion, she gave a housewarming tea party for a little Hyman contingent: her sister Betty and husband Ben, Annie's son Sam and his wife Phyllis, and my cousin Denise and her husband Bernard. Annie was by then in a nursing home and not well enough to travel across London to Chiswick.

Stella thrived in Homecross House and made new friends there. Sadly, other members of the extended Hyman family didn't fare as well: Uncle Ben died in 1991 and cousin Sam in 1992; Auntie Annie outlived her son by a year and died in 1993 in her late '90s. But if there were now no surviving Hyman husbands there were still two Hyman Girls and their children, and there is a set of photographs of very nearly all the remaining members of the clan in the family album, recording the most heartwarming of occasions: Stella's ninetieth birthday in October 1992.

Annie was still alive but not well enough to leave her nursing home in North London, and Pearl's daughters Irene and Hilary were still in America and Australia, where they had now lived more years than they had previously lived in England. But there, beaming and festive, are all the rest of us: Stella, with Rosalind, Derek and Gary, Audrey and me and Simon and Carey; Betty with her children: Denise and her husband Bernard, Nigel and his wife Marise, Lindsay and her husband Avi; cousin Derek with his second wife Andrea, cousin Andrew with his wife Jean; and cousin Sam's widow Phyllis.

It's a fine autumn afternoon; the caterers have fitted us all in on gold chairs round a long dining-table stretching diagonally across the sitting room at Park Road; the wine is flowing, the happy band of Hyman survivors and their loved ones are chatting and laughing. Phyllis, now an accepted matriarch herself, makes an unexpected little speech of appreciation. I, beaten to the punch, rise to make the expected speech, toasting my mother's health, and find myself helpless with laughter as I am prompted and "helped" by Phyllis and the day's third matriarch, Betty; and the sunny Birthday Girl presides over it all looking fifteen years younger than the ninety we are celebrating. It's a day to remember.

After almost exactly ten years in Homecross House, Stella began to suffer a number of accidental falls, both in her flat and outside it, necessitating emergency visits to Charing Cross Hospital – one of them for a fractured ankle – and it was clear that it was becoming increasingly difficult for her to look after herself unassisted. Rosalind and Derek carried out some extensive research on retirement homes in the St John's Wood area, roughly half way between Chiswick and Edgware, and found a pleasant little establishment in the Finchley Road called Spring Grove. In February 1995, when Audrey and I were going abroad on holiday and wouldn't be available for Stella's weekly shopping excursions or her now frequent phone calls for help of one kind or another, we took the opportunity to give her a little holiday of her own and moved her there as an experiment. Stella liked the place, the staff and the regime; so, two months later, we took her back to Spring Grove and made the move permanent.

Life in a retirement home was most agreeable for Stella to begin with. She was comfortable and well looked after; she could happily read her Daily Mail, play kaluki and exchange life stories with the other residents, make her own way into the dining room for her meals and join the Spring Grove coach parties for their occasional theatre and cinema excursions. Rosalind and I visited her alternately during the week and phoned her regularly between visits. From time to time, joined by Audrey and Derek, we took her out for lunch to Oslo Court or Lindy's in the Wellington Hotel. On Sundays and Christmas Days I'd collect her for lunch at Park Road. And in that wonderful March of 1996 when Nicola, Francesca and Isabella were born, Rosalind and Derek brought Stella over to Simon and Carey's flat in Philbeach Gardens to join us in taking turns to hold those precious little bundles.

Closing Chapters

By the time the girls had their Blessing Ceremony six months later, however, Stella was in a wheelchair: her physical balance was impaired and her mental balance was beginning, just slightly, to deteriorate. It wasn't consistent and it wasn't always obvious, but she was clearly becoming a little confused and delusional: "I'm a princess, you know", she told Rosalind on one of her visits to Spring Grove, "It's in the newspaper".

When Nicola, Francesca and Isabella were old enough to join us for lunch at Park Road in their high chairs, and later on, when they had begun to toddle and talk, they increasingly bemused her. "What's he doing now?" she would ask, as one of the girls tried to climb on her lap. She knew they were her great-grandchildren and they knew and still remember her as "Big Grandma", to distinguish her from Grandma Audrey; but there are photographs of the girls looking intently at Stella and Stella looking intently back at them, and you realise that it's a look of mutual, curious but baffled incomprehension.

Spring Grove suspected that Stella had had a number of tiny strokes which had affected her physically and mentally. By the beginning of 1998 she had become a little cantankerous and aggressive in her manner and the NHS medical inspector assessed her as suffering the early stages of Alzheimer's. In February she had a major stroke and was rushed into the Royal Free in Hampstead. We were all convinced that this was the end for her – Simon came to the hospital to make his last farewell; but the Hyman girls are fashioned of sterner stuff: if they make it into their 70s, they seem to be able to just go on making it, and Stella was now in her ninety-sixth year.

After six weeks in hospital she was recovered and ready to go home, but it had already become clear that she couldn't go back to Spring Grove: she needed the medical care and attention of a nursing rather than a retirement home. So Rosalind went off on her field trips again, looking for a suitable nursing home as conveniently sited as Spring Grove had been. After an intensive and dispiriting search – they might have been conveniently sited but the sights, sounds and smells of some of the nursing homes Audrey and I visited to confirm her assessments were discouraging in the extreme – Rosalind discovered Heathgrove Lodge, a few miles further up the Finchley Road. It was the happiest of discoveries. Heathgrove Lodge was efficiently run; the nurses and carers were capable and compassionate; Stella's room was small but light and airy, with French windows opening onto a balcony that overlooked the home's attractive garden; and the food was edible – an absolutely indispensable feature because her appetite would stay with her right to the end.

Stella thrived again at Heathgrove Lodge. The stroke had somehow dispelled her cantankerousness: she was mellow and genial, and grateful for the care and attention she was receiving. For a while the fantasies and delusions lessened too, and sitting in her armchair during the day she was capable of having a perfectly reasonable and good-natured conversation, especially about the past, although her memory was extremely foggy. I brought her some of the old photographs I was putting together for the family album in the hope that they might strike a spark. She loved the pictures of her gang strolling along the promenade at Southend but couldn't remember any of their names: she could only say "They're my friends". And heartbreakingly, when I showed her photographs of Dave in their courtship days and asked if she could remember who this young man was, all she could say was "No… but he's a good-looking boy".

The Hyman genes are remarkably tenacious. Betty, mute and bed-ridden for months in her nursing home in Finchley, died in 2006 not much short of her 99th birthday. For Stella, the decline was equally inevitable, but it was an even longer time coming. The carers would take her down to the restaurant for lunch or wheel her into the garden or onto her balcony when the weather was fine. Much of the rest of the time she would sit in her armchair and watch television, which became as real to her as the rest of her world. She spoke of people who'd been to visit her and talked about what they had been up to, but it didn't take us long to realise that these were characters in some soap opera she'd been watching. Rosalind and I alternated visits to give Stella lunch in her room, which she ate with her eyes fixed to the screen. Rosalind was feeding her on one occasion when Bob Monkhouse made a big entrance on his lunchtime quiz show, striding towards the camera with a big smile on his face and his arms outstretched, and Stella said "Brian's looking well today!"

Before very long she was too frail to be moved to her armchair and had to be confined to her bed. She still watched television, still ate a hearty lunch, was still happy to see us and have little conversations with us or with her carers; but gradually and steadily all these functions shut down. Some time in her 99th year Stella closed her eyes and stopped talking, a silent, wispy, white-haired little woman in a little nursing-home bed. But she still enjoyed her food: propped up against her pillow, soundless, eyes resolutely closed, her mouth would dutifully open to receive each spoonful, like a little bird.

Did she hear Rosalind and me in our separate visits chattering away, bringing her up to date with the family's activities, telling her the funny things her great-granddaughters had done or said? Was she conscious of our presence? Did she understand Rosalind and Derek when they told her that Gary had met a lovely girl and was going to marry her? Was she aware of Gary and Julie when they came to visit? Did she take in what we told her about their glowingly happy wedding day on 22 September, 2001?

I believe she did.

I believe that, with her eyes firmly shut – and lips too, except at meal times – her conscious or subconscious mind was somehow taking everything in. I believe it because of what happened on 27 October, 2002, the day of her 100th birthday. The family had agreed that Rosalind would call in to give Stella her lunch, wish her a happy birthday and congratulate her on her Birthday Card from the Queen; and Audrey, Simon and I would visit her in the afternoon to offer our own birthday greetings.

Lunch went extraordinarily well. Rosalind was moved to be joined by the nursing home carers – all of them extremely fond of Stella – who brought in a specially made birthday cake and sang Happy Birthday to that silent, unseeing, motionless little bird – who startled everybody by suddenly opening her eyes and smiling. It was only for a moment, and she didn't eat any of her birthday cake, but it was clear that she knew what was going on.

Audrey and I had arranged to meet Simon outside Heathgrove Lodge early in the afternoon so that we could go in together. Simon, driving north from Kensington, arrived on time. Audrey and I, coming from Chiswick on the North Circular, hit a huge traffic jam at the junction with Harrow Road. A tremendous storm the night before had flooded roads and brought down trees and traffic lights. The police had closed the North Circular at that point and were trying to divert the traffic back to Hangar Lane and up the Harrow Road; and it wasn't moving.

We phoned Simon to say he shouldn't wait for us: "Go in and say hello and tell her we'll be with her as soon as the traffic allows." We arrived two and a half hours later, Simon having long gone. I rushed up to Stella's bed – were her eyes just closed as usual or was she asleep? I kissed her on the forehead and burst into a long explanation for our delay: sorry not to have arrived sooner, last night's storm had created havoc, the roads were closed, the traffic was appalling… And suddenly, from the rusty depths of that tiny body, came the halting, croaky words "I…knew…you…were…coming."

They were the first words Stella had spoken for two years; and they were the last. On 5 June, 2004, five months short of her 102nd birthday, having fought off and rallied remarkably from a succession of chest infections, one final infection was too much for her and that stubborn little heart finally stopped. Seven weeks later, on 27 July, Julie gave birth to Christopher, and she and Gary transformed the lives of Rosalind and Derek by presenting them with their first grandchild. A new life for an old one; and an abiding remembrance of the past: Christopher's middle name is David, and he is named after his great-grandfather.

A Last Word, For Now.

I began this memoir in an attempt to capture as much as I could of the story of Stella and Dave, the Hyman girls and the Tesler men and women, before it faded from my memory. It was Simon who prompted it, when he realised that the rabbi who spoke about Stella's life at her funeral was far too young to have known any of it himself and must have been primed by me. "Well, now you should go home and write down everything you remember about Grandma and Grandpa before you forget it" he said. "Write about your own grandparents, about the East End, about your life as a child before and during and after the War: the girls will be fascinated by it, and so will I."

Whether he or the girls or any other members of the family who read it will in fact be fascinated, the story does cover a century full of incident, some of which is bound to seem strange to them. L.P. Hartley wrote at the beginning of his novel The Go-Between, "The past is a foreign country: they do things differently there"; and so we did. But so, too, will Nicola, Francesca and Isabella who, as Tesler girls, carry the story forward now themselves. How full of incident and adventure will that story be? Where will it take their lives? What careers will they follow? What kind of marriages and families will they have?

All I can say is that I hope they enjoy the ride, think of the children and grandchildren who will one day want to know each step of the journey they are embarking on, and don't make my mistake.

They should always remember: *Write things down!*

Brian Tesler
London, 2006.

Index

For the sake of space, this index is limited to the people mentioned, listed alphabetically by surname (although first names precede each entry). To keep family members together the women are for the most part listed under their maiden names, with their married names appended in parentheses.

T

W